"To say this book is full of gems here and there does not suffice. Rather, the entire text sparkles and shines, page to page, start to finish. It dazzles in both its scholarly rigor and pastoral care. Smith manages to pull off a rare feat: He cuts the biblical material with his exegetical incisiveness even while he comforts with his pastoral tenderness those marginalized and excluded by many in the church. Whether you hate Paul, or (like me) like him but only conditionally, this is your next book. Let Smith reintroduce you to the *real* Paul, a Paul who is much more authentic and compelling than the deformed one we unfortunately have inherited."

— José Francisco Morales Torres, Claremont School of Theology

"As an African American biblical scholar, I appreciate Smith's argument in *Paul the Progressive?*. Concisely moving through various texts in the Pauline corpus, Smith's work has wide-reaching implications for those of us who fight for liberation and justice within church and society. As a pastor himself, Smith provides a starting point for other pastors to teach and preach Paul in such a way that perhaps even Nancy Ambrose (Howard Thurman's grandmother) and other grandmothers like her (including mine) can envision a conversation around Pauline texts that do not delegitimize the humanity of formerly enslaved persons, women, and non-Jewish Christians, even as we seek to live lives that expand our contemporary views of Christianity."

— Angela Parker, McAfee School of Theology

"I have to admit that the apostle Paul has become one of my least favorite people in the Bible. Whereas I have seen Jesus as a figure that embodied ethical and social progress, my reading of Paul led me to believe that the apostle, in many ways, was regressive, and his writings have been used to marginalize and justify harm against so many people. However, in *Paul the Progressive?*, Dr. Eric Smith has presented a groundbreaking work that is both scholarly and accessible and that helps us to reframe our understanding of the teachings of Paul in order to see him as an agent of progress and social reformation on the issues that are at the center of our theological and public discourse today. Smith's work has helped me to begin reconciling my broken relationship with the apostle and has birthed in me a renewed interest in Paul's writings as tools to inspire and incite positive change in my own life and in my community of faith. If you're looking to be challenged, intrigued, and inspired, *Paul The Progressive?* is a must read!"

— Brandan Robertson, pastor of Missiongathering, San Diego, and author of *True Inclusion*

"I am a firm believer that every worshiping Christian deserves a chance to work out their faith in ways that make sense to them. We all need resources that are accessible and informative to get there. Eric C. Smith has done that on a subject much debated in Christian communities for ages: what do we make of Paul? If you have ever deliberated over whether Paul distorted or enhanced the core message of Jesus, you should add this book to your library. Whether you agree with his conclusions or not, you will appreciate his scholarship, find his writing style engaging, and be grateful for what he has added to a critical and ongoing debate in the life of the Church."

— John C. Dorhauer General Minister and President, United Church of Christ

PAUL THE PROGRESSIVE?

THE COMPASSIONATE CHRISTIAN'S GUIDE
TO RECLAIMING THE APOSTLE AS AN ALLY

ERIC C. SMITH

chalice
press
Saint Louis, Missouri

An imprint of Christian Board of Publication

Cover art: Medallion with Saint Paul from an Icon Frame,
    Gift of J. Pierpont Morgan, 1917
Cover design: Jesse Turri

ChalicePress.com

Print: 9780827231726   EPUB: 9780827231733   EPDF: 9780827231740

Printed in the United States of America

Dedicated to the people of

Biltmore United Methodist Church, Asheville, North Carolina

First Plymouth Congregational Church, Englewood, Colorado

Contents

Preface

If you ask progressive Christians about the Christian tradition, they will usually point to two moments where things went off the rails: the reign of the Emperor Constantine in the fourth century, and the career and writings of the apostle Paul in the first century. In both cases, progressive Christians will often talk wistfully about an otherwise-pure tradition that was sidetracked or co-opted. Constantine, the thinking goes, married the church to the state and sold out theology to imperial ideology. Paul, meanwhile, took the beautiful tradition Jesus left behind and turned it into an anti-woman, anti-gay, pro-slavery, anti-sex system of guilt and shame. If it had not been for those two moments, my fellow progressive Christians say, Christianity would be much better off today.

Those charges are a little bit unfair to Constantine (though that's a matter for another book), but Paul *definitely* does not deserve all the hate. After years of studying Paul within the academic field of biblical studies, I have come to see him as one of the most misunderstood figures of the Bible and the Christian tradition. And after years of preaching Paul in progressive Christian congregations, I have found that if he is read in light of modern biblical scholarship, we can legitimately understand Paul as an ally rather than an enemy. So much of what we *think we know* about Paul is *wrong*, and so much of what we *don't know* about Paul shows the apostle to be *far more right* than we imagined. On a litany of charges—misogyny, homophobia, anti-Semitism, xenophobia, prudishness, slavery apologetics, and oppressive theology—Paul's reputation has much more to do with centuries of bad interpretation than it does with Paul himself. Some of the worst things attributed to Paul are found in books that many scholars now believe he didn't actually write. Some of Paul's authentic writings have been taken out of context and had their meanings twisted. The Paul so many of us have hated isn't the Jesus-following Jewish Paul of the first century, but the Paul of Reformation-era figures such as Martin Luther and John Calvin. Peel back these layers of misunderstanding and bad interpretation, and a new Paul starts to emerge—or, actually, a very old Paul starts to reassert himself.

Not only have we wrongly considered Paul an enemy, but we have also missed out on an ally. The Paul that is revealed in careful study of his letters is nothing like the person so many progressive Christians hate, and, in fact, he shares many progressive Christian values. He's passionate about justice, honesty, reconciliation across difference, and inclusion most of all. He gets angry and indignant when people pridefully put themselves above others. He intervenes on behalf of those with less power, recognizes the leadership of women, and believes in a God who has thrown open the doors to welcome everyone in. At times Paul can be surly, petulant, thin-skinned, and proud, but the person who emerges from his letters is electrifyingly human and authentic, even at a distance of nearly two thousand years.

I wrote this book for the people I have encountered in churches across the United States: people who are progressive, who want to be faithful, and who are looking for models of progressive faithfulness. Pastors and laypeople alike understand that there is a deep connection between the Christian tradition and their values, but most of the oxygen in the room is taken up by more conservative kinds of Christianity, not to mention more conservative kinds of politics. In talking with these progressive faithful people, I have heard them talk about Paul as an enemy to be overcome or ignored. However, the Paul I have encountered in his letters would be delighted to join their cause. He was always getting chased out of town by the (pagan) religious conservatives of his day, getting yelled at by traditionalists of all kinds, and working to tell people about a better way. Paul went around proclaiming a God who was overturning old certainties, chipping away at old empires, and throwing open the doors to new family. He's much more naturally our friend than our enemy.

This book feels risky in a way that writing for an academic audience or writing a sermon rarely does. A book like this that crosses audiences and genres, and speaks out of and into different contexts, has the potential to ruffle feathers everywhere. In these pages, I have tried to strike a balance between saying too much and saying too little. Nearly every page could have had ten others behind it, tracking down opposing arguments, footnoting the history of the ideas, and presenting alternative scenarios. But this is not that kind of book. I have not always (as my math teachers used to say) "shown my work." Likewise, there are probably places where I have said too much, or said things too opaquely, because I could not find a simpler way to say them. And, at every turn, there are possible objections, different interpretations, or alternative readings. This is the nature of biblical interpretation: no one framework explains everything, so we are left to try to find the explanations that can clarify the most. Paul himself is not always clear or consistent, and many parts of Paul's letters allow for multiple competing interpretations.

And of course, my own identity, location, and experiences limit my perspective. I am a straight white man, and a Protestant Christian with advanced degrees in religion and biblical interpretation, which gives me a view of Paul that's different from the view others have. Without a doubt, the limitations of my perspective will be evident in this book, and I hope that by presenting my perspective I do not limit the perspectives of others. As Paul himself seemed to recognize, communities benefit when every person contributes.

It also feels risky to be so openly confessional. Although all of my professional life has included both congregational ministry and the academic study of religion, those two worlds rarely meet. A scholar of religion who is religious can be accused of lacking objectivity, while a religious person who studies their own religion can be accused of lacking spirit. I suspect that I am guilty and innocent on both counts, and in this book I make little attempt to hide behind objectivity—not that there is such a thing. Instead, I try to help my two worlds talk to each other, but mostly I try to help the academy talk to the church, because I believe it has a lot to say about Paul.

My favorite verse of all of Paul's letters is Galatians 6:11: "See what large letters I make when I am writing in my own hand!" This bit of trivia delights me. Paul had been using a scribe to dictate his letter, but at the end he took the pen and finished it out, as a personal touch and a mark of authenticity. But Paul was not a professional scribe, and his handwriting was bad, so he made light of how crudely he wrote in his own hand. That's how this book feels to me. I have written it in my own hand, however inelegantly, and now I give it to you, the reader. I hope you will find something worthwhile in it.

Acknowledgments

This book was made possible by the questions, struggles, teachings, and truths of hundreds of people over the past decade and a half. Some of those people were my students, some were my teachers, some were my congregants, and some were my friends and colleagues. It would be impossible to name them all, but I owe a debt to every person with whom I have discussed Paul, the New Testament, and the Bible generally.

The people of two congregations I have served deserve special mention. Biltmore United Methodist Church in Asheville, North Carolina, was my first ministerial position, and that congregation helped form and shape me in powerful and durable ways. I remember especially a number of wise elder mentors from that congregation—Jayne Smith, Naomi Wray, Joyce Anderegg, Martha Strunk, Esther Megill, Doris Gidney, Ray Ferell, Elaine Gasser, Carlos Rodriguez, John Reed, Lorraine Gribbens, and of course Ashley Crowder Stanley, to name only a few—who helped me grasp how biblical studies, congregational ministry, and progressive values intersect and inform each other. Then, for over the past dozen years plus, First Plymouth Congregational Church in Englewood, Colorado, has helped me understand what a stridently progressive congregation can be, and it has helped me sharpen my ideas through countless conversations, sermons, classes, and discussions. Without those two churches, this book would not exist.

I also owe thanks to my students and colleagues at the Iliff School of Theology, who have formed the rich community of interpretation out of which this book has grown. These students are remarkable individually and as a group, and I am more hopeful for the world when I think of them in their many callings in the church, the nonprofit sector, and in society.

I am grateful to several individuals who read parts of this manuscript and offered helpful feedback, including Julie Muñoz Pittman, Jason

Koon, Jeremy Garber, Dorcia Johnson, Suzanne Marie Myfanawy, and many others who expressed an interest in the project and supported it in various ways. Dennis Haugh was especially insightful in pushing me to clarify aspects of my thinking, and to draw a distinction between different traditions of scholarship and my own thinking.

The First Plymouth Endowment generously awarded me a grant to fund a retreat to write part of this book, and I am grateful for their support in this and other projects. When that writing retreat on the North Carolina coast was interrupted by Hurricane Florence, I evacuated to the home of my mother Dorothy Smith, and I am grateful to her for providing me the space to keep working.

My deepest gratitude is to my wife Jessa Decker-Smith and my three children—Amos, Hazel, and Eli—who give light to my life.

CHAPTER 1

Hating Paul (An Introduction)

"I Kind of Hate Paul."

"I kind of hate Paul." In almost every Bible class I've ever taught in a church or in a seminary classroom, someone has said these words of the person whose name is on about half of the books of the New Testament. They usually say it in a way that tells me that they know they're not *supposed* to hate Paul. With a nervous grin on their faces and a "please don't be angry about this" tone in their voices, dozens of people have told me that they cannot stand one of the most important figures in the history of Christianity.

People are usually relieved when I smile back. Not that I hate Paul—I don't—but I certainly understand why people do. Most of my circles are filled with progressive Christians, and progressive Christians seem to hate Paul much more often than their conservative sisters and brothers do. Progressive Christians can usually recite a laundry list of reasons why they hate him, but most people seem to have one particular reason for why they hate Paul. For some, it's because of all the passages in Paul's writings that condemn homosexuality—and, usually, these Christians turn out to be people who have been wounded deeply by other Christians using Paul's words against them. For others, it's because of Paul's contempt for women and women's leadership. Often, these are women who have had their calls to ministry squashed, challenged, or undermined by their communities—and their gifts devalued—because of words that Paul wrote. Still others have a particular disgust for Paul's sexual ethics—the way he always seemed to be shaming people for having bodies and wanting to derive pleasure from them. Some see Paul as a defender of slavery. Others point to Paul's anti-Semitism as their most important reason for hating him, often citing personal connections to the Jewish faith and the ways Paul's anti-Jewish words have been used to hurt people they love. Recently, some people have a new reason to hate Paul—after his writings were used to defend the separation of families detained at the United States' southern border. And, perhaps most frequently of all, people will talk about the way Paul took the message of Jesus—a message of peace, love, forgiveness, and community—and turned it into a system of personal salvation full of guilt, debt, and unpayable obligations to God. These people have often escaped fundamentalist or conservative Christian childhoods, in which the writings of Paul were used to instill feelings of inadequacy, shame, and (to use a word from the writings of John Calvin) *depravity*. For many Christians like this, Paul was the hijacker of Christianity, the person whose writings mark the point at which the tradition went from beautiful to abusive.

I've encountered so many Paul haters in my New Testament courses that I now begin class with a stark confession of my own: I love Paul. I don't always *like* Paul, but I *love* Paul. I think Paul has gotten a bad rap. More than that, I think Paul has been completely misinterpreted by the Christian tradition. The Paul we know (and hate) has almost nothing in common with the Paul we encounter by taking a fresh look at his letters. I love Paul, I tell my classes, because once you get past centuries of Christian interpretation of him and approach Paul on his own terms, he turns out to be endearing and sneakily liberal. He turns out to be passionate about what he believes in, and he gets angry when he thinks people are being deceitful or dishonest. He can be stunningly egalitarian, a supporter of women's ministries, and nothing at all like the misogynistic Paul we usually imagine. Instead of being anti-Semitic, he is one of the proudest defenders of Judaism in antiquity. Almost every reason to hate Paul listed in the previous paragraph turns out to be mostly unfounded if you look at the writings of Paul himself. Once you get to know Paul on his own terms, and get rid of the things the church has piled onto his shoulders over the years, most of the reasons to hate Paul go away, and what's left is a Paul who is inspiring, moving, and actually very progressive.

I know: you don't believe me—yet. Most of my students don't either, in the beginning. Often they'll say that they're open to being convinced, but they're obviously skeptical. That's understandable given how the church has used and misused Paul over the years, and how much damage that misuse has done. But by the end of the course, many of my students have gained a grudging respect for Paul, and some even love him as I do. A few continue to hate Paul, but in my experience the more you're able to strip away layers of Christian theology and doctrine and encounter Paul in his own voice in the writings he left us, the more you like him.

It turns out that the Paul most of us know isn't the real Paul. Most of us know a Paul who's an invention of generations of interpreters and theologians, so encrusted with the residue of creeds and bad interpretations that he's hard to recognize. We know Paul through isolated verses pulled out of context, or we know him through books that bear his name that he didn't actually write. We know Paul through sermons about hellfire and those dramatic, "If you died tonight, where would you go?" ultimatums, although Paul never asked anything that sounded like that. We know a Paul that has passed through the filter of two thousand years of Christian thinking, but those twenty centuries of thought have made Paul into something he never meant to be. And, if we can get past *that* Paul, to the *real* Paul that we meet in his letters, we will find a very different person there waiting for us.

Ground Rules for Reading Paul

This book is an attempt to convince you to think about Paul differently. I hope that I can convince you that Paul was *not* a misogynist, a homophobe, an anti-Semite, a prude, an apologist for slavery, a defender of arbitrary government power, a purveyor of spiritual debt and guilt, or a hijacker of the Christian tradition. I hope I can introduce you to a Paul who was early Christianity's great champion of inclusion, constantly pushing the boundaries of how people thought about God's family. I want to convince you that Paul was a champion of women, working alongside women and holding them up as examples of faithfulness. And, I want to persuade you that Paul was a Jew, and a proud one at that, and by no means an enemy of Jews and Judaism. By looking at the way Paul thought about ethics, I want to show that Paul was not a supporter of slavery, that he never meant his words to be used to instill shame about sex, and that he would object strongly to having his writings used to defend the separation of families at the border. I want to demonstrate that Paul was a great pilot of the Christian tradition, not its hijacker, and that the ways Paul's words have been used to create theologies of guilt and debt have nothing to do with Paul himself.

But before we do all that, we need to set some ground rules about how to study Paul's writings and other New Testament writings about Paul. These ground rules come from modern biblical scholarship and the many tools it uses to analyze texts. Not all scholars would agree with all of these, but through years of research and teaching about the Bible, these are the ones that I have chosen. There are four ground rules:

1. Know that Paul didn't write everything attributed to him.

2. Trust Paul's own words over the words of others about him.

3. Trust Paul's actions as evidence of his commitments.

4. Recognize that we are always already viewing Paul through a particular theological and historical lens.

Together, these four ground rules will help us to sift through the evidence found in the New Testament and come closer to the truth about Paul. They aren't foolproof, but they will give us a road map through Paul's life, teachings, and writings. I'll say a bit more about each of these ground rules, giving some context for them and why they are helpful.

Paul Didn't Write It All

First, it's important to realize that Paul did not write everything that has his name on it in the New Testament. This can be difficult for some people to hear, because it challenges their notion of what the Bible ought to be. It's hard to accept that there might be dishonesty canonized in the pages of the Bible. But in the ancient world, it was not uncommon for works to be written under someone else's name, and it wasn't always dishonesty, exactly. Often the followers of an important figure would write works using that person's name after their death as a way of furthering that legacy or of "completing" that work. The book of Isaiah is a good example of this; scholars believe that the "original" Isaiah wrote only chapters 1–39 of the book, and that one or more additional authors, inheritors of his tradition, wrote the remaining 27 chapters using Isaiah's name.[1] It also happened with other ancient writers, who sometimes complained even in their own lifetimes about people writing in their name, a stranger making a buck off their reputation.[2] But with Paul, it probably didn't happen until after he had died, and it was probably done by people with good intentions, who only wanted to claim some of Paul's authority to make a point with which they thought Paul would have (or should have) agreed. This seems really shady to us today, and it violates our ideas about intellectual honesty, but in antiquity it was fairly common, and sometimes it was even honorable.

There are 14 books sometimes associated with Paul. Of these, we can dismiss one right away. The book of Hebrews, which is sometimes called

---

[1]Michael D. Coogan, *A Brief Introduction to the Old Testament* (New York and Oxford: Oxford University Press, 2009), 271–72.

[2]For a good and broad account of ancient forgery, see Bart D. Ehrman, *Forgery and Counterforgery: The Use of Literary Deceit in Early Christian Polemics* (Oxford: Oxford University Press, 2013).

"Paul's Epistle to the Hebrews," isn't by Paul (and it isn't an epistle, for that matter; it's probably a homily), and it doesn't even claim to be written by Paul. His name's attachment to it is just laziness; the book is part of the same section of the New Testament as Paul's writings, so it gets lumped in with the rest. Of the remaining 13 books, scholars are unanimous about Paul's authorship of only seven of them: Romans, 1 Corinthians, 2 Corinthians, Galatians, Philippians, 1 Thessalonians, and Philemon. It's hard to find a Bible scholar who disputes that Paul wrote those; it's as close to a sure thing as there is in the study of the New Testament.

The remaining six are subject to varying levels of debate. Colossians, Ephesians, and 2 Thessalonians are sometimes called the "disputed" epistles or the "Pseudo-Pauline" epistles, because there is significant disagreement among scholars about whether Paul wrote them or not. Generally speaking, more theologically conservative scholars tend to think Paul did write them, while non-Christian or liberal Christian scholars tend to think he didn't. Beyond theology, the differences of opinion come down to how much importance you give to things such as vocabulary and style. These three letters differ from the seven undisputed ones in important ways. Reading them in the Greek, you can tell that there are big changes in the word selection and even in the sentence structure when compared to Paul's undisputed writings. There are also differences in theology; 2 Thessalonians, for example, has a very different view of the timing of Jesus' return than 1 Thessalonians and Paul's other writings. Of course, a person's writing and theology might change over time, and that is a major argument made by people who think Paul *did* write these books. I am one of those who thinks that these three books were probably *not* written by Paul, although there are sections of them that sound a lot like Paul, and that might preserve authentic traditions of Paul's sayings or even snippets of Paul's writings. But generally speaking, we can't count on these books to tell us much for certain about Paul, and when determining Paul's positions on things I set these aside. In this book, though we will look at passages from some of these books, we will always view them as non-Pauline works.

Titus, 1 Timothy, and 2 Timothy are often called the "Pastoral Epistles," and it is more broadly (but not unanimously) agreed that Paul didn't write these. They are called "Pastoral" because they all have an emphasis on pastoral ministry; they are all written from the standpoint of an elder "pastor" or missionary giving advice to a younger one, using Paul's name as the elder. There are many reasons to think that these don't come from Paul himself, including the same reasons of style, word selection, and theology that we saw with Colossians, Ephesians, and 2 Thessalonians. But, there are other reasons too. The Pastoral Epistles seem to assume a church structure that didn't yet exist in Paul's day; 1 Timothy, for example, spends a lot of time talking about church offices, such as bishop and deacon, that didn't fully develop until a later time.[3] Although Paul's undisuted letters sometimes mention deacons (like Phoebe), these mentions always presume an informal kind of leadership, as opposed to the Pastoral Epistles' presumption of a more organized and standardized hierarchy of church offices. In all likelihood, these letters come from a time well after Paul's death, and were written in his name as a way of offering advice to future generations of church leaders. That certainly makes them useful, but they can't tell us much about Paul himself, and these too we have to set aside. Again, I'll reference some of these works in this book, but always with the assumption that Paul didn't write them. I sometimes tell my students that it's helpful to think of these works as "fan fiction." They are tributes to the "original," and in some ways they participate in the same universe as the "original," but they exist outside the boundaries of what the "original" author imagined or set forth. As with fan fiction, these books can still be useful and even entertaining, but they aren't *Paul*.

Of the fourteen works commonly attributed to Paul, then, we have to limit ourselves to only half: the undisputed (or "authentic") letters. These range from majestic and sophisticated letters, such as Romans and 1 Corinthians, to a messy and chaotic letter such as 2 Corinthians. Philemon, the shortest of them all, is hardly a spiritual letter at all, although it will play an important role in chapter 6 of this book. In some of these letters, Paul is deferential and submissive, hoping to gain favor from people with authority and resources. In others, Paul is angry and defiant, having been challenged in his ministry and finding himself needing to defend his reputation. His language is sometimes meandering and confusing, and sometimes wildly poetic. Although we are limited to only seven letters, these seven letters present us with a portrait of a complex and fully human person, and they are enough to draw some conclusions about Paul and his interests, desires, ideas, and character.

There is one more aspect to this first rule, though. Even once we have limited ourselves to the seven undisputed letters of Paul, we still have to be careful in how we read them. That's because of two complicating factors. The first is that Paul wrote letters instead of essays or treatises, and letters require special care in reading. And the second

---

[3] See for, example, 1 Timothy 3:1–13.

is that a great deal of time has passed since Paul lived and died, and his writings have been handed down to us in ways that might have changed the texts themselves.

This first complication is a question of genre. Genre is very important to understanding any written work; we need to know what kind of text it is before we can begin to interpret it. For instance, if you approached this book you are holding in your hands as if it were a cookbook, you'd likely be very confused, and you'd make some mistakes of interpretation. If you're reading this paragraph through the genre of *cookbook,* it probably doesn't make much sense. You won't do much better if you read it as an example of the genre of *science fiction.* But if you understand the correct genre, you understand the rules of reading the text, and you'll have a head start on interpreting it.

All of the writing we have from Paul is in the form of letters. These are formally called "epistles," and they follow the letter-writing conventions of Paul's day. Most of them start and end in roughly the same way, and Paul follows a series of stepping stones as he writes them: he starts with a salutation, names the addressee, gives a brief thanksgiving, proceeds to the body of the letter—where he lays out what he wants to say—then adds an exhortation and a concluding greeting of some kind. This form varies a bit from letter to letter— the lack of a thanksgiving in Galatians 1 is a famous and powerful example, showing that at that moment Paul very pointedly *did not* give thanks for the Galatians—but generally speaking Paul always writes the same way. Knowing that this is how Paul is writing can help us to see different emphases and omissions in the texts; if Paul rushes through or lingers on a section, this might be important and may signal we should pay particular attention to that section.

But beyond that, it's important to recognize the basic fact that what we're reading is a letter. As far as we know, Paul never sat down to write out his thoughts in any systematic way. He wasn't writing works of theology, ethics, or Christology. He wasn't trying to cover everything he thought or believed. Paul's letters are one part of a larger correspondence between him and his churches (or, in the case of Philemon, between him and a friend, and in the case of Romans between him and a church he wanted to visit). They presuppose a broader relationship beyond the letter, and they are always "occasional," meaning that Paul had a particular reason, or occasion, for writing them. So, while a modern theologian might write an essay on salvation, and try to explain in it everything she knows and thinks about salvation, Paul never did anything like that. Instead, Paul was always responding to the living and breathing communities that he knew—their crises, challenges, failures, promises, and possibilities. Everything we have from Paul's pen was pastoral, in that sense. All of his letters were meant for real, living people who Paul knew or wanted to know. When we read Paul, the saying goes, we are reading someone else's mail. Paul's letters were never meant for people like us, and Paul probably would have been affronted at the idea that people would be reading his notes to the Thessalonians—much less reading them *as scripture*—twenty centuries later. He didn't mean these writings to apply to all people, always and everywhere. He meant them for the people to whom he addressed them. We always have to read them with that limited scope in mind.

The second complication is that the letters of Paul have taken a long and winding journey to get to the pages of our modern Bibles, and the form in which we have them might not reflect the form in which Paul wrote them. They were probably kept as treasured items by their recipients, and gradually copied and shared with other communities. Eventually, Paul's letters started circulating as a collection; the modern order of the letters—longest-to-shortest, with the exception of the "seconds" (2 Corinthians, 2 Timothy, and 2 Thessalonians)—developed as a way to fit them all into a single book. They were copied and translated over centuries, and many scholars believe that they were altered during that time. Some of these alterations are easy to spot and explain: some scribes misspelled words or copied a line twice. However, others are far more complicated.

The case of 2 Corinthians is a good example of how complicated things can get. Most scholars agree that 2 Corinthians is a composite letter, made up of at least two letters of Paul's that were combined (out of order) to make the letter we have today. You can see the evidence of this in the transition from chapter 9 to chapter 10; the language goes from joyful and thankful to angry and hurt, without any explanation at all. This is likely because two or more letters have been spliced together to make a single document without smoothing out the tone and themes between them. We don't know why this was done, but in order to understand Paul's words in that letter we have to untangle some of the mess.

A different kind of alteration can be seen in 1 Corinthians 14:33b–36, the famous (or infamous) passage in which Paul instructs women to be silent in church. We will look at this passage more closely in chapter 2 when we talk about Paul and misogyny. But, for now, try reading 14:26–40 *without* verses 33b–36, and notice that the passage still makes a lot of sense—and maybe more sense—without those verses. Notice that those verses contradict what Paul has already said in the letter in 11:5, in which Paul seems to assume that women are praying and prophesying regularly in the community. They are hardly being silent. Notice, if your Bible includes it, the note that some ancient manuscripts of 1 Corinthians don't include these verses here at all, but instead put them at the end of the chapter, after verse 40. All of those factors together have convinced some scholars (including me) that verses 33b–36 are a later addition to Paul's letter, dropped in by some scribe after Paul's death to bolster that scribe's own opinion against women holding leadership positions. If this is indeed the case, then they don't belong to Paul himself, who—in contradiction to this passage—in this same letter and elsewhere in his writings assumes and even defends women's work in the Christian tradition. There are several instances similar to this in the New Testament, and while it might offend us to think of someone tinkering with the Bible, identifying these inserted passages is critical if we are to understand Paul in his own words.

Together, these two complications make the job of reading Paul a little trickier—but far more enjoyable, in my opinion. This is because it turns out that some of the most offensive parts of Paul's letters either weren't really written by Paul at all, or were written for such specific circumstances that we shouldn't try to apply them to our own contexts today. This is not to explain away or relativize Paul's words, but simply to recognize them for what they were and are: teachings for particular people in particular times and places that we encounter by reading someone else's mail.

Trust Paul's Own Words

Beyond Paul's letters (and other works attributed to Paul but probably not written by him), there is another major source of information about Paul in the New Testament. The book of Acts is a *kind* of history book, tracing the beginnings of the church from the time of Jesus' death until the middle of the first century. While the first half or so of the book is about Jesus' disciples and their activities in and around Judea, the second half of the book turns toward the life of Paul. Three times it describes Paul's experience on the road to Damascus, when a dramatic flash of light and a voice from heaven interrupted his life and caused him to become a follower of the dead-and-resurrected Jesus.[4] Acts then goes on to describe Paul's missionary life, tracing his journeys across the Mediterranean and Aegean Seas, and through Asia Minor, Greece, and ultimately to Italy, where the story abruptly ends with Paul awaiting an audience with the emperor.

A book such as Acts, with nineteen chapters more or less devoted to Paul's story, would seem like a great boon to our understanding of Paul and his thought. However, there are some serious problems with using Acts as a source for knowing the real Paul. The central problem

---

[4]Acts 9:1–22; 22:4–16; and 26:9–18.

is that Acts was not written by Paul, and it seems to tell Paul's story in a way that conflicts with the way Paul tells it in his own letters. Many scholars agree that the author of Acts is the same person who wrote the Gospel of Luke, and this person seems to have been a pretty decent historian; at the beginning of both Luke and Acts, the author takes a step back to comment on his own writing and his own place among different accounts. But, there are significant differences between Paul's undisputed letters and Acts' account of Paul's life. For instance, Acts describes Paul's missionary technique in a way that doesn't look anything like what Paul does in his letters. In Acts, when Paul gets to a new city, he visits the synagogue there and preaches about Jesus to the Jewish community. Inevitably, in Acts, he is thrown out of the synagogue, and only then does Paul go and recruit gentiles. But in Paul's own letters, he doesn't describe things this way. Instead, Paul arrives in a new city and sets up shop as a leatherworker or a tent-maker (the Greek is ambiguous), and through the contacts he makes in that business he sets up a social network and works within that to evangelize. So while Acts has Paul first approach Jews, get rejected, and only then recruit gentiles, in Paul's own letters he goes straight to the gentiles—and he calls himself an "apostle to the gentiles" (Rom. 11:13). This is a pretty significant theological difference, because it goes to the question of the status of Jews in Christianity, which we will consider further in chapter 4.

Another dramatic example of Acts disagreeing with Paul's own account is found in the story of his Damascus road experience. Acts tells the story of the aftermath of Paul's experience, and how afterward Paul went to Jerusalem to visit with the disciples who were there. Although Acts is never very clear about the timing of this visit, the implication is that it follows quickly after the Damascus road experience, and that it represents a kind of "reporting for duty" in which Paul, newly recruited to Christianity, shows up at headquarters. The home office, then, "sent him off to Tarsus" in Acts 9:30. The inescapable conclusion is that the Jerusalem apostles were directing Paul's activities, deploying him where they saw fit. In this model from Acts, Paul is a kind of franchisee of the Jerusalem church. But, that franchise model is very different from how Paul himself describes his embrace of Jesus and its aftermath. In fact, Paul almost seems to know the story as Luke tells it (even though Acts probably was not yet written when Paul was writing his own letters), and he reacts angrily against it. When he tells the story in Galatians 1:13–24, Paul doesn't mention any miraculous flash of light or voice, and he makes a very big deal out of insisting that he was *not* taking orders from the Jerusalem apostles. "I did not confer with any human being, nor did I go up to Jerusalem to those who were already apostles before me, but I went away at once into Arabia, and afterwards I returned to Damascus." (Gal. 1:16b–17). Paul seems to have heard the story that Acts tells—that he was taking his orders from Jerusalem—and he wants to state emphatically for the record that he was answering God's call independently: "Then after three years I did go up to Jerusalem to visit Cephas and stayed with him fifteen days; but I did not see any other apostle except James the Lord's brother... [A]nd I was still unknown by sight to the churches of Judea that are in Christ" (Gal. 1:18–19, 22). Here, Paul is stridently staking out his independence. In the middle of that passage, he interrupts his own story: "In what I am writing to you, before God, I do not lie!" (v. 20).

I believe him. I think Paul was telling the truth in this part of Galatians, and in other places (such as in 2 Corinthians 10 and 11) where his authority had been challenged. Paul's pride could be a hindrance to him, but here it makes me believe what he's writing: he is telling the truth, and he simply cannot believe that someone would be telling an untrue story about him. Paul had a very keen sense of self and a very well-formed way of seeing himself in the world, and he was genuinely affronted when someone misrepresented him.

This is the basis of the second ground rule for this book: we should trust what Paul says about himself more than we should trust what others say about him. This is particularly true of Acts, which was likely written some time after Paul's death, and wasn't meant to be a work of history in the modern sense. The author of Acts was telling the story of Paul in particular ways, for particular theological and narrative purposes. It isn't "objective" history, and it was never meant to be. The story in Acts is told from a specific point of view, and that point of view was different from Paul's own. When Acts conflicts with Paul's own writings, which happens with some regularity, we should trust Paul. Paul was writing during his own lifetime from the best possible vantage point for describing his own actions, and Acts was written a generation or more later by someone who might or might not have known Paul, but who certainly did not know Paul's experiences as Paul himself did. When the two conflict with each other, trust Paul's own words.

Trust Paul's Actions

The old saying goes, "actions speak louder than words," and, in the case of Paul, this can be a helpful way to sort through the sometimes-contradictory things that he wrote and that were written in his name. Because, as pointed out earlier, Paul's letters were all occasional—meaning they were written because of particular circumstances or occasions—Paul's teachings in his letters are always specific to the contexts to which he was writing. He never meant for his letters to be read by people everywhere as general guides. When we read these letters today, as people living many centuries later and in very different contexts, it can sometimes be hard to sort through what Paul means.

The example of 1 Corinthians 14:33b–36, discussed earlier in this chapter, is helpful. In that passage, Paul appears to instruct women to be silent in church. There are very good reasons to believe that Paul didn't write these verses, but probably the main reason is that they don't fit with what we know about Paul's communities. We can already see, earlier in 1 Corinthians, in 11:5, that Paul seems to assume that women are *not* being silent in church. Rather, women are being heard in church plenty—they are praying and prophesying in the Corinthian church, often enough that Paul feels compelled to mention how they should dress while doing it. This means that there was a practice of women participating in and even leading church services in Corinth—a congregation that Paul himself founded. Here, the words about women in worship in 14:33b–36 are at odds with what Paul and his communities actually did in worship. We should trust Paul's actions.

There are other examples of this in Paul's letters, many of which we will get to in later chapters. In Romans 16:1, Paul gives a short recommendation for a woman named Phoebe, who was probably the person delivering the letter to the Roman churches. He calls her "a deacon of the church at Cenchraea," which was the port town that served Corinth. Phoebe, then, was probably a kind of clergy person (though the categories of clergy were still a little fuzzy in that time) in one of Paul's own churches—again, showing us that Paul was perfectly fine with women in leadership. Later on in that same chapter, in verse 7, Paul refers to someone named Junia, who was "prominent among the apostles." Junia is a woman's name, and the fact that Paul was naming a woman as one of the apostles was so "scandalous" that, for centuries, scribes and translators assumed that Paul had meant to write "Junias" instead, a man's name, and changed the biblical text to make this person a man. But, as I will argue in chapter 2, Paul didn't make a mistake; he was perfectly comfortable calling a woman an apostle.

There are other examples of this kind of thing, where Paul's actions are important signs of what he thinks is true or valuable. His missionary strategy tells us that he didn't think of salvation in the way most modern Christian theologies think he thought about it; we will talk about that more in chapter 8. His repeated statements about his own Jewish identity, and the way that identity continued to play out in his life long after he had his experience of Jesus on the Damascus road, tell us that Paul lived his life as a Jewish person and as a Jesus-follower; we will talk more about that in chapter 4. Paul's proposed solution to the problem of a runaway slave, found in the short letter of Philemon, tells us that while he probably didn't oppose slavery outright, he did try to work for liberation and even justice and reconciliation between slaves and slaveholders; we will talk more about that in chapter 6. Paul doesn't talk much about his personal life, but what little he reveals tells us something about his reasons for some of his teachings on sexuality and ethics more generally; we will talk more about that in chapter 5. Across a range of questions, Paul's own actions can tell us a great deal about his beliefs and understanding of Christianity, and sometimes these actions and practices can be an important corrective to mistaken ideas that come from misreadings of Paul or from texts that Paul didn't write but which appear in his name.

Paul, after all, was a very practical person. He wasn't interested in grand theologies or religious systems. Paul was interested in action, because he believed that there wasn't much time left. This is key to understanding Paul's ethics: Paul thought that he was living at the end of time, and that Jesus' life, death, and resurrection meant that God was about to draw history to a conclusion, or at least dramatically shift the way the world worked. Paul thought that this might happen during his lifetime, so he had a frantic energy about him. Paul thought that the salvation of the gentiles depended on his mission; he thought that there, at the end of time, God had charged Paul personally with bringing the gentiles into the family of God. Like a harvester working feverishly before the first hard frost, Paul was laboring under a deadline, and so his actions tell us what was most important to him, and what he thought was true about Jesus and about God's plan for the world. There was no time for complicated or pompous theologies; time was short, and action was all that mattered. Paying attention to *what Paul did*, then, tells us a lot about what he thought was true—as much as, or more than, what Paul wrote.

Recognize Our Own Lenses

The fourth of these ground rules for reading Paul might be the most difficult: we have to recognize that we are always already viewing Paul through a particular theological and historical lens. In other words, Paul is not a stranger to us. We already know *a version* of Paul, whether we've read his letters or not. As people living in a world in which Christianity is a powerful force, we have grown up knowing something about Christianity and assuming some things about Paul's role in it. And, in certain forms of Christianity—Protestantism in North America and Europe, in particular—Paul's role in the Christian story has been especially large. The problem is that *the way* Paul's part in the story has been told, *especially* by Protestants, has distorted Paul's own words in powerful and harmful ways.

There is a saying that it takes at least a generation for an idea to make its way from the academy to the pews. I think that might be optimistic. Once scholars have changed their minds about something, or discovered something, or begun to view an old idea with a new emphasis, it takes a new generation of ministers going through seminary, graduating, getting jobs, and preaching and teaching that idea for a decade or two before the idea really becomes common among laypeople. This isn't because laypeople are slow learners or apathetic Christians; it's just because ideas take time to proliferate. We saw this in the 1980s and 1990s with scholarship on the Historical Jesus; it took a generation for the ideas and conclusions of groups such as the Jesus Seminar to become really common among regular churchgoers in progressive churches. Even today, a generation later, Historical Jesus scholarship is commonplace in some churches and unknown in others.

Something similar has been happening with the study of Paul over the past generation of scholarship. Beginning in the 1970s and 1980s, and really gaining steam over the last quarter-century, there has been a revolution in the study of Paul.[5] In some ways it's even more dramatic than the story of Historical Jesus scholarship. Scholars of Paul have almost completely torn down the study of Paul and Paul's letters and rebuilt it from the ground up. But, you'd never know this from listening to sermons at most churches. In the academy, there has been a great overturning of ideas about who Paul was, what he believed, and why he matters, but it has been almost completely absent from churches.

This new perspective on Paul is called just that—the "New Perspective on Paul"—and it is contrasted with the old perspective, usually called the "Traditional Perspective on Paul" or the "Lutheran Perspective on Paul," after the most famous and influential architect of the old theory, Martin Luther. This book is an attempt to translate the idea of the New Perspective (and especially a variety of it that some people call the Radical New Perspective) for the church, and especially for the progressive church, so we will spend a lot of time on it in the chapters to come, especially chapters 4 and 8.

But, before we do that, it's important to spend a few minutes thinking about the Traditional Perspective (or Lutheran Perspective),

---

[5]Many people date the beginnings of this movement to the publication of an essay by Krister Stendahl in 1976: Krister Stendahl, "Paul and the Introspective Conscience of the West," in *Paul Among Jews and Gentiles* (Philadelphia: Fortress, 1976), 78–96.

because the Traditional Perspective functions like the default operating system of Christianity. Even if you've never heard about the Traditional Perspective or thought very much about Paul at all, there is a very good chance that the assumptions you have about Paul come directly from the Traditional Perspective. And, there is a very good chance that, according the findings of the New Perspective, most of those assumptions are wrong. The default "software" is outdated and very, very buggy. Or, to return to the metaphor of lenses, the glasses through which we see Paul are blurry and cracked, they distort the view, and they are well overdue to be replaced.

The Traditional Perspective is sometimes called the "Lutheran Perspective" because it was the view of Paul held by Luther, who popularized it and helped "install" it as the default operating system of the emerging Protestant churches. Luther himself was working from older readings of Paul, dating back to Augustine in the fourth and fifth centuries, so in some ways this is an old reading of Paul. But, in other ways Luther was innovating around Paul, making certain aspects of Paul's letters more important than they had been, and making Paul himself more central to Christianity as a whole. Luther's distinctive emphases and assumptions became the default emphases and assumptions for enormous swaths of Christianity, and they have remained that way until today.

Luther's theology is a broad and complicated subject, and we don't have time or space to cover it all here. But, a few distinctive aspects of it should be enough to show how much Luther has influenced our ideas about Paul, and how much those ideas about Paul have come to stand in for Christianity as a whole. First and most significantly, Luther understood Christianity as a religion concerned with personal salvation. This happened, for him, through a process called justification by faith. In this way of thinking, faith in Jesus, which is both an intellectual assent and also a commitment of the spirit or heart, is what "saves" us. For Luther (and many other Protestants), this was contrasted to "works," the idea that we could *do* things to achieve our own salvation. Luther, remember, was a "protestant" against the Western Christian tradition (often called the Catholic or "universal" tradition), and so he was arguing against things such as acts of penance—and *especially* the sale of indulgences—as useful means of obtaining forgiveness for sins and achieving salvation. Whether Luther's characterization of Catholic practice was fair or not (my answer: yes *and* no) is a subject for another time, but his emphasis on faith-and-not-works became the linchpin of his theology.

Luther thought Paul supported this position. Following Augustine, Luther understood Paul as a tormented soul, bound up in a system of works-righteousness (Judaism, in Paul's case, in a characterization no fairer than Luther's characterization of Catholicism) and in desperate need of personal salvation. Luther understood Paul's experience on the road to Damascus as a turning point in Paul's life, when Paul became a Christian by believing that Jesus was his savior. Paul rejected Judaism, the Traditional Perspective goes, and turned toward Jesus as the founder of a new religion. He spent the rest of his life trying to convince others of the same: first Jews, but when they rejected the message, gentiles also.

The Traditional Perspective is more complicated than that, but you can probably already fill in some of the blanks yourself. If you've ever encountered Christian evangelism, the chances are good that it followed a path a lot like that one: recognize that your own attempts to live a righteous life have been a failure; accept Jesus as savior, knowing that his death was payment for your sins; live as a Christian, reading your Bible and praying daily, and spreading the word about salvation to others. This is often called the "Romans Road" to salvation, because a lot of the Bible verses on which it's based can be found in Paul's letter to the Romans. This was how Christianity was presented to me as a child and a teenager, and it's how I was expected to present it to others when I worked at an evangelical summer camp. It was the only way I knew Christianity to function; I couldn't conceive of any other kind of Christianity, or any other reading of Romans or the rest of Paul's letters. This was what Christianity *was* for me—with faith in Jesus at the center—and perhaps you're nodding your head along in agreement as you read this. We'll look at all of this more closely in chapter 8, but you get the general idea.

The New Perspective overturns most of this by taking off those Traditional Perspective glasses and looking at Paul's writings with fresh eyes. What would happen, Bible scholars started to ask, if we read Paul on his own terms, instead of assuming that everything Paul wrote would fit into the tidy categories of a theological system that wasn't fully devised until 1,500 years after Paul died? It turns out that Paul's own writings don't support the Traditional Perspective very well at all. It's true that in most Bibles you'll find phrases such as "faith in Christ" and "justification by faith," but many scholars are now not nearly as confident as they used to be that those phrases mean what the Traditional Perspective thinks they mean, or even that they're translated correctly. We'll talk more about this in chapter 8, but, generally speaking, the New Perspective understands Paul's writings to be describing something that is both simpler and more complicated than the Traditional Perspective describes. In the New Perspective,

Paul doesn't "convert" to Christianity, since there was no Christianity to convert to. Instead, Paul, who was Jewish, *stayed Jewish,* and incorporated into his Jewish identity a belief that another Jewish man, Jesus of Nazareth, was critically important to the plan of (a Jewish) God. Likewise, Paul didn't reject all those things that Luther dismissed as "works-righteousness," such as keeping dietary laws and circumcision. Paul still thought they were really important—if you were Jewish. However, most of the people in Paul's Christian congregations weren't Jewish, they were gentile, and, for gentiles, keeping Jewish law—trying to be Jewish—was a mistake. Paul wasn't suggesting abandoning works; he was suggesting abandoning the misguided attempt to hijack someone else's identity. In other words, Paul wanted gentiles to stay in their lane.

Likewise, under the New Perspective, salvation isn't all about the individual. Paul wasn't the first in a long line of converts to Christianity. Instead, Paul was one of the first to recognize that the life, death, and resurrection of Jesus—what Paul summarizes as "Christ, and him crucified" in 1 Corinthians 2:2—was a decisive moment in the history of God's interaction with the world. It was the moment, coming near the end of history, when God had opened up the family of God to the gentiles. God had not abandoned the Jews, as Luther and so many other Christians have so often assumed. God had a covenant with the Jews, and God doesn't break covenants. Instead, in the life, death, and resurrection of Jesus, God was doing a new thing that offered hope of salvation to *everyone else,* and it was Jesus' faithfulness to his calling and mission that had made it happen. It goes beyond the evidence found in Paul's letters to say that Paul was a universalist, believing that everyone would be saved. But, I don't think that's far off, and I think if we could ask Paul today to explain his meaning, he might say something that sounded suspiciously universal. Jesus was, for Paul, not a "gotcha" moment in which salvation depended on saying yes to a strange proposition ("faith in Christ," or "accepting Jesus as your personal lord and savior"). Jesus was, for Paul as read in the New Perspective, the moment when God threw open the doors and invited everybody in. Paul thought his job was to go and tell the gentiles the good news.

How to Stop Hating Paul

Speaking of good news, I hope this book comes as good news to all the people who have told me that they "kind of hate Paul." Again and again, I've heard this from progressive Christians, but I hope this book helps some of them to see Paul in a new light. People have so many reasons to hate Paul—some personal, and some systemic. Some of us can't tolerate his misogyny or his homophobia. Some of us are put off by his anti-Semitism, by his prudish sexual ethics, or by the way his writings were used to justify slavery or enforce nationalist xenophobia. And, some of us just think his theology was bad, and that it infected the rest of the Christian tradition with a system built on guilt and shame. There are lots of reasons to hate Paul, and very few reasons to give him a second chance.

I know, because I used to hate Paul too. I hated him for all of those reasons above—especially the misogyny and homophobia. I hated him so much that I rarely even read Paul unless I had to, and even then it was with a roll of my eyes or a dismissive tone in my voice. However, as I began to study Paul seriously during my doctoral work, and as I began to preach from Paul's writings regularly in the progressive Christian churches where I worked, I began to encounter a new Paul—one I had never met before. And, I discovered that most of the reasons I had for hating Paul weren't good reasons at all. If anything, they were reasons to be angry at people who had misrepresented Paul to me over the years, writing things in his name that he would never have said, and overlaying his writings with theological agendas and systems that he would never have recognized. I learned to stop hating Paul, and to start hating what people had done to Paul. And, more than anything, I learned to love Paul as an ally in progressive Christianity—as someone who was one of the first in the Christian tradition to fight for inclusion and justice, to honor and promote women's leadership, and to spread the message that God was doing a new thing.

In this book we will take on, one by one, all of the reasons why we hate Paul. One by one, we will discover that our hatred has been misplaced, and that, in some cases, it has been exactly wrong. Paul was not an anti-Semite; he was, and remained, a proud Jew. He wasn't a silencer of women, but instead he assumed their leadership and recommended them to others. He didn't create a complicated system of salvation based on faith in Christ; he thought that in the last days God had thrown the doors open for all to come in. Paul was a progressive in every sense of the word; he saw himself as an apostle of the one who had changed everything, sent to those on the outside looking in. He had seen a vision of what God was doing in Christ, and he couldn't rest until everyone else could see it too.

CHAPTER 2

Paul the Misogynist

Freshman Orientation

When I arrived on campus for my freshman year of college, I was greeted by something I had never encountered before: a female campus minister. By the time I made it to college, I had become very involved in a congregation in my hometown, which I now know was part of a denomination that ordained women, but in the rural area where I lived I had never actually met a female minister, and I don't recall having heard that such a thing was possible. I had spent most of my teenage years deeply immersed in evangelical Christian subculture, where there was never any suggestion that women could lead congregations. Most of the books I read at the time, and the music to which I listened, came from evangelical Christian bookstores, and none of them even mentioned the possibility that ministers could be women or women could be ministers. The college I had chosen was affiliated with the Southern Baptist Convention, which was then (as now) associated with conservative Christian ideas. So, it was a surprise when I got to campus and was greeted by the campus minister, an ordained Baptist woman named Paula Dempsey.

It was a surprise, but it was a pleasant surprise. Rev. Dempsey was in charge of the pre-orientation retreat of which I was a part, so we got to know each other quickly. She was a patient woman, since many of the students at the college, like me, were encountering women in church leadership for the first time. She was an excellent pastoral presence and more than a little prophetic—I suspect she had to be, as a woman in her position. In my evangelical youthful zeal, I once wrote a column for the school newspaper criticizing the decision to use female language for God in the Lord's Prayer in a chapel service, and Rev. Dempsey's response was as gracious as could be imagined. We sat down and talked about it, and she used what might have become a conflict to redirect my thinking on the subject.

A few years after I graduated, Rev. Dempsey was relieved of her position. I don't know all the details of why she was let go, but the Southern Baptist Convention had recently shifted its policies on women's ordination, and, while the school was by that time in the process of distancing itself from the denomination, perhaps the pressure from a heavily Baptist alumni community and local religious leaders proved too great. To those of us who were loyal to Rev. Dempsey (and by then I was definitely one of those), it was a great loss, but it was only one of many such cases in which women found their ordinations and their jobs in jeopardy. Something had shifted over the course of a few years, and many of those women whose communities had affirmed their calls were suddenly being told that they *weren't* called by God— not to be ordained ministers, anyway.

The conflict over women in ministry isn't the only place where Paul's ideas are in conflict with progressive understandings of gender, though. There are places in writings attributed to Paul in which the author gives advice to women and men about being in relationships. Two parallel passages in disputed epistles, Ephesians 5:22–33 and Colossians 3:18–21, give explicit instructions to couples: "Wives, be subject to your husbands." These verses are part of longer sections of those letters in which the author is giving practical advice about different kinds of relationships—between parents and children, and between slaves and slaveholders, in addition to relationships between husbands and wives. There is much in these sections that is disturbing, and that has been used to justify the subjugation of women over the years. Modern scholars' doubts about whether Paul wrote these passages hasn't stopped many Christians from interpreting them as gospel truth, and using them systematically to oppress women.

This is one of the big reasons that people hate Paul: because they think he was a misogynist. The ideology behind so much—behind some Christians' insistence that women cannot be in ordained ministry, and behind traditional gender roles in marriage—can be traced back to the apostle Paul. Or, to be more accurate, it can be traced back to people's *ideas* about Paul, and to many texts that *claim* to be written by Paul, but probably weren't. Most of the debate about women's roles in church leadership and family life doesn't come from Jesus, who never said much on the subject. Most of the debate about women's roles comes not from letters attributed to Paul, but letters (or sections of letters) that he probably didn't write. Here, two of the ground rules we discussed in the previous chapter are really important: know that Paul didn't write everything attributed to him, and trust Paul's actions as evidence of his commitments. Let's follow these rules while looking at these passages about women, and see where they lead us. We'll start with some of the passages about women from letters attributed to Paul but probably *not* written by him, then we will move on to passages about women that probably *were* written by Paul, and, finally, we will look at the way Paul seems to have understood and treated women who were Christian leaders in his own day.

Pseudo-Paul's Problem with Women

Scholars sometimes call the author(s) of the disputed letters of Paul "pseudo-Paul." In our day, when "fake news" has become a catchphrase, it might be better collectively to call these people "Fake Paul." Pseudo-Paul—or, in actuality, several pseudo-Pauls—probably wrote about half of the letters attributed to the apostle: 2 Thessalonians, Ephesians, Colossians, 1 Timothy, 2 Timothy, and Titus. It's no coincidence that some of the most troublesome passages about women come from these pseudo-Pauline letters, and *not* from the letters that all scholars agree Paul wrote.

The composition dates of these disputed letters are the subject of a lot of argument among scholars, but generally speaking they are dated very late by people who are convinced that Paul didn't write them. Most often, these letters are given dates in the late first century or early second century, but, indications are that Paul died sometime in the early '60s. So these letters would have been written a generation or two *after* his death—most likely by people who were trying to claim his authority to speak to the issues of their own day. While this practice seems dishonest to us, it really wasn't very unusual in that time. In all likelihood, these letters were written by someone who wanted to speak with the voice with which they imagined Paul would have spoken if he were still alive, to address questions that simply hadn't come up during Paul's lifetime.

This was an urgent need by the late first and early second century, because much had changed since Paul's day. While Paul, as an apocalyptic thinker, had expected Jesus to return very shortly, by a generation or two after Paul's death, it was becoming clear that the second coming would be delayed. Christianity had continued to spread through the Roman Empire, and some Christians became interested in setting up church structures and systems that could last, since it appeared that the new religion would have to persist a while before Jesus' return. As communities of Jesus-followers entered their second or third generations, church leadership that had once been figured out on a case-by-case basis became more formalized. In practice, this meant that Christian communities started to look similar to other religious movements around them, which often meant that they became more patriarchal in terms of leadership. As Christian communities slowly shifted out of private homes and away from shared communal meals, women's roles slowly faded into the background. In the same way, family gender roles had been shifted, ignored, or abandoned in the heady days when Christians had expected the end of the world to come soon, but after a few generations they snapped back into line with the family gender roles that were common in the Mediterranean world. Christianity was changing to meet changing times, and some Christians thought that what the church really needed was Paul's opinion on things. Hence, pseudo-Paul.

Ephesians and Colossians are two of the disputed Pauline letters—or, to put it simply, they are two of the letters that many scholars believe were written by pseudo-Pauls. These two letters share a lot of concerns in common, and, on the subject of women's roles, they sometimes speak with a curiously similar voice, as noted earlier. Ephesians 5:22–33 and Colossians 3:18–19 are part of larger sections that scholars sometimes call "household codes," because they give advice to people who are living within household systems. In every case, the "household codes" assume a hierarchy between the parties, and they call for obedience on the part of the "inferior" parties. Slaves were inferior to masters and therefore should obey them; children were inferior to parents and should obey them; and wives were inferior to husbands, and should obey them—at least according to Ephesians and Colossians. These letters argue for the status quo of the time, not for the leveling of hierarchies and overturning of boundaries taught by Jesus and advocated by Paul.

The household in Mediterranean antiquity was almost always a patriarchal affair, dominated by men and male prerogatives, and so it's no surprise that, when Ephesians and Colossians dispense advice on the subject, they do so in patriarchal ways. "Wives, be subject to your husbands as you are to the Lord," reads Ephesians 5:22. "Wives, be subject to your husbands, as is fitting in the Lord," says Colossians 3:18. In both cases, the call for wives to be subject to husbands is followed quickly by admonitions for husbands to love their wives. Some modern Christians point to this as evidence of balance or equality between husbands and wives, and others see it as outlining distinct gender roles within marriage—with husbands loving and wives obeying.[1] But loving

---

[1] One version of this is called "complementarianism," and it argues that scripture lays out different but complementary roles for men and women. Cherith Fee Nordling, "Gender," *The Oxford Handbook of Evangelical Theology* (Oxford: Oxford University Press, 2010).

is not quite the same thing as being subject to, and this double standard is a major reason that progressive Christians hate Paul.

There is no getting around the fact that these passages were written by a very early Christian person, but there is good reason to doubt that the person in question was Paul. The vocabulary and style of the letters differ from those of Paul's undisputed letters, and even when this pseudo-Paul uses the same concepts that the real Paul does, pseudo-Paul uses them in different ways. The focus on household life is a sign that these letters come from a time *after* Paul's own lifetime—a time when Jesus' return was not so immediately expected, and when family and gender roles were shifting back toward social norms. A dozen or so parallel passages between Colossians and Ephesians—such as the one about wives being subject to their husbands—suggest that both of these documents were part of a larger pseudo-Pauline tradition.[2] The authors of Colossians and Ephesians seem to have been creating their letters by taking words and phrases from some of Paul's authentic letters, from tradition, and from other pseudo-Pauline materials, and recombining them to make new letters with some of the characteristics of the old ones. They were doing this because they thought that something needed to be said about a number of issues, including the role of women, and that it needed to be said with the authority of Paul's voice. It worked, because even today, nineteen centuries later, Christians still appeal to these passages as a scriptural warrant for women's subordination to men. This is one of the reasons that people who value gender equality hate Paul.

But the writings of pseudo-Paul, those falsely attributed to the real Paul, are at odds with something that Paul says about marriage relationships in his undisputed writings. In 1 Corinthians 7:2–7, Paul outlines a much more egalitarian view of marriage, defined by mutual accountability. This passage is troublesome for other reasons, as we will see in chapter 5, but it shows us that Paul himself, when writing about marriage, didn't have the instinct to subordinate women to men. While Paul himself was likely unmarried (as 1 Corinthians 7:8 suggests), in the writings that we can confidently assign to Paul he never subordinated wives to husbands. He explicitly described marriage as an equal partnership. In fact, Paul seems to have known one or more couples quite well, and, in the closing chapter of 1 Corinthians (16:19), he mentions one of them: Aquila and Prisca. Prisca (or Priscilla, as she is known in Acts) is one of several women with whom Paul had a working relationship. To understand more about how Paul regarded women's

---

[2]A list of the parallel passages is available in Amy-Jill Levine and Marc Zvi Brettler, eds., *Jewish Annotated New Testament*, 2d ed. (Oxford: Oxford University Press, 2017), 411.

roles in early Christian communities, we will turn in a moment to her story, and the stories of other women leaders in the early church, and to the way Paul thought about the women in church leadership he encountered and with whom he worked. But, before we do that, we need to look at a few more passages from Paul's writings—this time, from letters that scholars concur the apostle did write, and see what they can tell us about Paul's attitudes toward women in ministry and family life.

Women in Corinth

Already in this chapter we've looked at a couple of different passages from 1 Corinthians in which Paul wrote about women. In 7:2–7, Paul describes marriage in egalitarian terms, and in 16:19 he mentions Prisca as someone who has a church organized in her house. But, two other passages from this important letter will help us to think about Paul's reputation for misogyny and whether it's deserved or not. First Corinthians 11:2–16 and 14:33b–36 both discuss women and their roles within worshiping communities, but they talk about them in very different ways. The differences between these two passages, even though they are found in the same letter, will help us to understand Paul's messy legacy on women in ministry. Beyond that, these passages will help us see how, even within Paul's undisputed letters, there might be more to the story than we think.

First, 1 Corinthians 11:2–16 is a confusing passage. It is obviously about men and women and their roles, but it is also about much more than that. In these verses, Paul is very concerned about hairstyles and head coverings, and he is outlining ways to think about worship leadership within the Corinthian community, and, perhaps most confusingly of all, Paul is worried about "the angels" and the effect the uncovered heads of women might have on those heavenly beings. The overall sense of the passage is that Paul wants to draw clear distinctions between the way women and men should look when they pray or prophesy. Men, Paul thinks, should pray and prophesy with their heads uncovered, but women should do so with their heads covered, "because of the angels" and because women are a "reflection" of men, who are a reflection of God. And, somehow, all of this has to do with angels.

With so much going on in this passage, it is difficult to get a clear sense of what Paul wants his readers to take away from it. Is he trying to make a general point about men and women and their relative nearness to God? Is he trying to contend with some particular situation in Corinth with regard to men and women praying and prophesying, perhaps settling some dispute within the community there that we no longer understand? Is Paul just making casual commentary about worship attire? This is the difficulty of trying to read and interpret ancient letters; we only have Paul's side of the conversation, and we aren't always fully aware to what conflicts or questions Paul was responding in his writing. It's possible that the question of women's attire while praying and prophesying was especially troublesome in Corinth for some reason that we don't know. If so, we might be on shaky ground if we try to universalize these verses to all women everywhere. On the other hand, if Paul really did mean to make a grand commentary on gender roles in this passage, and we dismiss it as a local dispute that happened twenty centuries ago, we might miss out on something valuable that Paul had to tell us.

One thing that isn't really hard to see in this passage is that *Paul assumed that women were praying and prophesying in Christian communities in Corinth,* and that they would continue to do so. Paul had no problem with this whatsoever; his real concern was with what their heads looked like while they were doing it. Nowhere in these verses does Paul question whether women should be leading worship experiences in Corinth, including in verses 7–9 where Paul is saying some pretty androcentric things about humanity. Even when Paul is claiming that woman was made "for the sake of man" and "woman is the reflection of man," Paul takes for granted that women are equal in the work of worship leadership. Recall that, when Paul's words are unclear on something, we should always look to his actions to help understand them. Here, Paul's actions speak volumes: in Paul's churches, women prayed and prophesied right alongside the men.

My own best guess about what is going on in 1 Corinthians 11:2–16 is that Paul was trying to settle a dispute in Corinth. The dispute probably started as a disagreement over cultural norms; notice that this section begins by talking about "traditions" that Paul handed down to the community in verse 2, and it ends by talking about "custom" in verse 16, so it's framed by appeals to tradition and to the habits of the community. By this time, Paul's Jesus-following communities were already overturning some social patterns and reconfiguring others, and perhaps some women thought—very reasonably, to our twenty-first–century minds—that following Jesus meant that old gender distinctions such as head coverings no longer mattered. Other people, however, insisted on tradition, and wanted those heads covered. Paul was trying to intervene to settle the dispute, because Paul's priority was unity and peace in his churches. His intervention took the form of reminding people why it had been traditional for women to cover their heads in the first place.

There are echoes of Eden in his explanation, where in one of the Genesis creation stories the first woman was made from one of the first man's ribs. Paul was appealing to scriptural authority here to reinforce an older gender rule, but at the same time he was affirming the equality that women and men have before God. Elsewhere, Paul says that "there is no longer male and female" (Gal. 3:28), and that's the idea he's driving at here too. Paul is traditional enough that he thinks men and women should dress differently for church, but he's progressive enough to know that women could and should pray and prophesy as well as men. Nowhere in this passage is that principle ever in doubt.

The question of the angels, and what they're doing in this passage, is a little harder to settle, although Genesis might once again give us a clue. In Genesis 6:1–4, "sons of God" take notice of the beauty of human women, marry some of them, and produce hybrid offspring. With his comment on "the angels" in 1 Corinthians 11:10, Paul might be referencing this bit of lore that is embedded in Genesis. It's the kind of thing that most Christians skip right over, or else dismiss as a belief belonging to a different time. If we can let go of or ignore a passage about lustful angels, then we can probably also move past the gender hierarchies that Paul uses in this passage. The takeaway here is that when it came time for the community to gather in Corinth, Paul expected women to be up front prophesying and praying alongside the men, and he never said anything in this passage that suggested that those Corinthian women shouldn't fill that role.

Later in the same letter from Paul to Corinth, this question of women in worship comes up again. If you are reading through the fourteenth chapter of 1 Corinthians, you'll be following Paul's comments about prophecy and prophetic gifts. Paul has been building up to this throughout the letter; his comments are connected to chapters 12 and 13, where Paul has discussed spiritual gifts and the cohesive bonds of love. In chapter 14, Paul again takes up spiritual gifts, but especially prophecy and the gifts of speaking in tongues and interpreting tongues. But, then, in 14:33b–36, something strange happens: the letter abruptly changes tone, and a few verses interrupt Paul's words about prophecy. These verses are among the most controversial in the letters of Paul, especially among verses that deal with the status of women, so they are worth reproducing here:

> As in all the churches of the saints, women should be silent in the churches. For they are not permitted to speak, but should be subordinate, as the law also says. If there is anything they desire to know, let them ask their husbands at home. For it is shameful for a woman to speak in church. Or did the word of God originate with you? Or are you the only ones it has reached?

This is, to use a technical biblical studies term, *weird*. It's weird for a few reasons. For starters, it doesn't seem to flow out of what Paul had been talking about before verse 33 or what he goes on to talk about after verse 36. It's related, of course—both these verses and the verses surrounding them have to do with things said out loud in churches. But, up until this point Paul had been talking about orderliness in worship, seemingly trying to alleviate some competition and congestion in Corinthian church. He had specifically mentioned the benefits of broad participation in worship in 14:26–28. Now, in these verses, he suddenly switches away from this inclusive vision, and he categorically begins to exclude broad classes of people! These verses are not exactly out of place in the chapter, but they don't exactly fit, either.

What's harder to account for is the fact that 33b–36 directly contradicts what Paul said a few chapters earlier in 11:2–16. There, Paul *assumed* that women could pray and prophesy in church; the only question was what they would be wearing when they did so. Here in chapter 14, there seems to be a blanket ban on women speaking in church at all! We know from elsewhere in Paul's letters that he knew and affirmed many women who were active in church communities. These women—whom we will meet in the section below—were deacons, coworkers, apostles, church founders, and trusted allies. Surely they did not all stay silent in "all the churches of the saints." Something else must be going on with these verses.

Many scholars suspect that what is going on with these verses is that Paul never wrote them. If you have certain translations of the New Testament, you can see some evidence for this in the text itself. The NRSV, for example, puts all of this material in parentheses, to show that it doesn't really fit with the rest of the text, and to show that Paul might not have written it. There is evidence from ancient manuscripts that these verses sometimes appear elsewhere in the text of 1 Corinthians, a sure sign that ancient scribes were uncertain about them, or that they had multiple texts that handled these verses in different ways. Such practices are often the biggest piece of evidence that something was added to a text later, and, in fact, that is what many scholars think happened here. This is called an interpolation, or an insertion into a manuscript. The idea is that later on, after Paul's death, a scribe or some other person added 33b–36 to Paul's letter to try to get his own position heard. He didn't think women should speak in church, and he thought that the way to get people to agree with him would be to have Paul say it for him.

This is really just a different version of pseudo-Paul. It's a little messier and more difficult here, because the pseudo-Paul words are embedded in the middle of a bunch of real-Paul words, and it can be hard to sort out the differences. But there are really good reasons to think that Paul never wrote these words about women being silent in church, being subordinate to men, and asking their husbands any questions they might have. These words don't fit with the rest of the letter, and they don't fit with what we know about Paul's behavior and attitudes toward women in his ministry. These women, if they could speak to us today, might well speak up on Paul's behalf, defending him from the slanders of the pseudo-Pauls. It's time we met some of these women.

Phoebe, Prisca, Junia, Chloe, and More

In both the introduction to this book and earlier in this chapter, I suggested a principle for thinking about how to understand Paul: we should trust Paul's actions as evidence of his commitments. The New Testament is full of words written by and about Paul, and those words can tell us a lot about Paul and his churches. Even the pseudepigraphal letters—the ones written by someone else in Paul's name—can tell us something about Paul and the way people remembered him after his own lifetime. But the information we can get from those words is limited, because when we read Paul's letters (and letters falsely attributed to Paul), we are reading someone else's mail. These letters were not meant for us; we are looking over the shoulders of the people for whom the letters were intended, and doing so at a distance of many centuries. Paul never imagined people like us reading his letters, and we don't know everything that his intended audience presumably would have known. Because of this, Paul often fails to explain or contextualize things in his letters, because he assumes that all of his readers will know what he's talking about. The example from 1 Corinthians 11 that I gave earlier is a great one; Paul assumes everyone knows why he's writing about the way people dress, so he doesn't bother to explain it. Because we are reading with only partial understanding and context, Paul's meaning in his writings (and the meaning in writings by others that are falsely attributed to Paul) is not always easy to interpret. Some passages from these letters that appear to be straightforward can turn out to be more complicated, and some parts of the letters are simply mysterious, given the gaps in our knowledge.

But there is sometimes more to the text of Paul's letters than we first realize. Beyond Paul's big theological points or troubleshooting of the communities he founded, we can find a different kind of material in Paul. Between the lines of the text, we can sneak glances at the world in which Paul lived, the people he knew and with whom he worked, and the way he went about his life and his ministry. These are not always things that Paul has set out to tell his readers, exactly, although they sometimes are. Usually these are offhand comments, names dropped in a long section of "shout-outs," or short descriptions of people and moments. These small moments can tell us a great deal about Paul and his commitments, even when he has not said anything explicit about them in his writing. For, in these small candid moments Paul reveals a lot about his attitudes toward women, and the ways in which women were his close colleagues, supporters, and sisters in faith.

One good example of these between-the-lines places is Romans 16, a chapter in which Paul is sending greetings to a number of people he knows in the city of Rome. Scholars are actually divided on the question of whether Romans 16 was originally part of the letter or not; some think that this final section of shout-outs was added later or attached by accident, or that the letter itself was a letter template sent to different cities, and we have the Roman version of it, with all of Paul's particular greetings to people he knew in Rome.[3] My own belief is that this list of greetings belongs with the rest of the letter as a coherent whole, since these kinds of greetings fit with Paul's purpose in Romans, through which he was trying to garner support for his missionary work to Spain. In this way of reading Romans 16, Paul's long list of greetings functions as a kind of contacts list for him—or maybe like Facebook's "People You May Know" feature, which Paul is using to show how much he and the Romans already have in common. This chapter is a gold mine for scholars who are trying to reconstruct the makeup of the earliest churches in Rome, since Paul mentions so many people by name. Scholars can tell a lot from these names and what Paul says about them: whether people were enslaved or free, whether they were men or women, from what ethnic background they might have come, what kinds of economic means they might have had, and what roles these people might have played in the early Christian movement. This is called *prosopography*, and it helps us as we try to understand the world in which Paul lived and the ways in which he understood his relationships with other Christians.

The first person mentioned in Romans 16 is a woman named Phoebe. The first two verses of the chapter are a short letter of recommendation for Phoebe, but even in this one sentence we learn a lot about Paul and how he thinks about Phoebe. He uses two important words to describe her: *deacon* and *benefactor*. Scholars dispute the precise meaning of both of the original Greek words from which these are translated; a deacon can be the name of a church role (a category of clergy, in Christian

---

[3]Robert Jewett, *Romans: A Commentary*, Hermeneia–A Critical and Historical Commentary on the Bible (Minneapolis: Fortress, 2007), 8–9.

tradition), or it can be a generic name for a person who helps others with a task. Paul uses the word in both ways in Romans; in 11:13 he describes his own work using it. There's good reason to think that in 16:1 Paul means something particular by the Greek word for *deacon,* because he calls her "a deacon of the church at Cenchreae," which suggests a special function with relation to that community. The second term he uses for her, translated "benefactor," helps explain this. The Greek word here is *prostatis*; it has a legal meaning of "one with authority," and a less formal meaning as "a person who is a patron of others." Phoebe, it seems, was a person of some financial means, and she had likely helped to support Paul and others with monetary help. Some scholars have argued that the church in Cenchreae even met in Phoebe's house, making her the benefactor and patron not just of Paul but of the community itself.

The purpose of Paul introducing Phoebe this way was probably because she was the one who was carrying the letter for him. There was no postal service in the ancient world, so someone wishing to deliver a letter usually sent it along informal networks. A letter writer might send it with a friend who was going in the general direction he needed the letter to go, and that friend would then pass it along to someone else at the next port town, and then that person would find someone going to the particular town to which the letter needed to go, and so on. Paul seemed to be taking a more direct route: he had entrusted the letter to Phoebe, who was carrying it on his behalf and presenting it to the churches in Rome. The fact that Phoebe could travel so freely adds to the likelihood that she was financially well-off, and the fact that she was chosen to represent Paul to Rome means that she was a person with a lot of status with Paul and the community in Cenchreae. In these two verses at the beginning of chapter 16, Paul is introducing Phoebe to the Romans, and giving her a recommendation. He is asking the recipients of the letter to receive Phoebe also, and to help her with whatever she might need.

Despite the rhetoric of the pseudo-Paul found in the section inserted into 1 Corinthians at 14:33b–36, despite that found in the letters to the Ephesians and the Colossians, and despite Paul's confusing language in 1 Corinthians 11:2–16, here we get an honest glimpse of the way Paul understood women's roles in the early Christian community, and the way he himself treated women. Paul understood Phoebe as a deacon of a local church, which is *at least* a complimentary way to describe her as a servant, and most likely an early example of a clergy role within the congregation. He identified her as a benefactor, calling attention to her own patronage of his ministry and the ministries of others. He likely entrusted the letter to Phoebe, giving her authority to carry it to Rome and to answer for it on his behalf. In other words, Paul held Phoebe in very high esteem, worked with her closely, and treated her as an equal (and, in some ways, superior) partner without batting an eyelid.

The very next verses, 16:3–5a, mention another woman: Prisca, or sometimes Priscilla. We've already had occasion to meet Prisca in this chapter, as an example of an equal marriage partnership with her husband Aquila, and as a rebuttal to the idea that Paul expected Christian women to be quiet and subservient. In the New Testament, Prisca is always mentioned alongside Aquila. In four of the six times they are mentioned, though, it is Prisca who is mentioned first. Here in Romans 16:3, Paul mentions Prisca first, which might suggest that she had a higher status or importance than her husband. In these verses, and in 1 Corinthians 16:19 where they are also mentioned by Paul, he speaks very highly of Prisca and Aquila as hosts of a church in their house, and as "fellow laborers" or "coworkers" with Paul who "risked their necks for my life."[4] These are hardly the kinds of words we would expect from Paul if he were the kind of misogynist we meet in the pseudo-Pauline writings. This is not a Paul who expects women to shrink into the background and ask their husbands their questions. Here we see Paul engaging with Prisca as an equal, putting her on equal footing with her husband (or higher), and acknowledging that Paul personally owes her a debt of gratitude for her work.

Just a few verses later, in Romans 16:7, we meet yet another powerful woman whom Paul praises as an important person in the new Christian tradition. "Greet Andronicus and Junia, my relatives, who were in prison with me," he writes; "they are prominent among the apostles, and they were in Christ before I was." This verse has been somewhat controversial in the past, but not because there was any dispute about the *status* of the people mentioned, for "prominent among the apostles" is just about the highest importance someone could have in early Christianity; instead, the very identity of the people mentioned became the subject of a messy historical mystery.

We are probably supposed to understand Andronicus and Junia as a couple, since they are mentioned together as other couples are (including Prisca and Aquila just a few verses earlier). In that way of reading the verse, Andronicus and Junia are Paul's relatives (either biologically, or in the sense that all three persons are Jewish), and they were followers of Jesus before Paul was, giving them an additional kind of prominence. The fact that they were imprisoned with Paul is also a status marker, showing that they were fellow sufferers with him. But being called *apostles,* and prominent ones at that, is very special praise.

---

[4]The NRSV translates Romans 16:3–4 as "Greet Prisca and Aquila, who work with me in Christ Jesus and who risked their necks for my life."

That is probably why some copyists and translators made a subtle but important change to the manuscripts at this point. They didn't change the title of "apostle," or any of the qualifications or accolades. Instead, they changed a name, turning "Junia" into "Junias,"—in the process, making her into a man.

The argument here relies on the Greek, so I won't go into it too deeply.[5] Basically, there are two ways to read the name in 16:7: as a woman's name in the accusative, or as a man's name. The woman's name, Junia, was a very common one in the ancient world, while the man's name, Junias, is otherwise unknown. Scribes and translators, though, especially from the medieval period onward, often assumed that no woman could possibly be an apostle, and opted for the male name Junias, even though that name didn't seem to exist in the ancient world. In doing this, they erased Junia from Paul's letter, replacing her with a man who was, supposedly, better qualified to be an apostle— simply on the basis of his gender.

This is a good example of how later interpretation has changed the way we understand Paul. By making this subtle change in interpretation—really a translation choice more than anything else— the Christian tradition let medieval and modern assumptions about women's roles in the church erase an apostle. Where once Romans had Paul enthusiastically sending greetings to a woman who was "prominent among the apostles," many Bible translations now have an invented man in her place. This is a good reminder that all translations and all editions of the Bible are already interpretations, with layers and layers of decisions already made for you. Even if the translators and editors are well-meaning, and even if you trust them, it's important to do your homework.

There are other important women in Paul's writings too.[6] In 1 Corinthians 1:11, we hear about Chloe, who seems to the head of a household whose "people" had reported back to Paul about divisions and discord in the Corinthian church. Chloe, similar to Phoebe, might have been a woman of some status and means. Two other women, Euodia and Syntyche, were part of the church in Philippi and seem to have been arguing with each other, causing Paul to urge them to get along in Philippians 4:2. The fact that they were disagreeing in such a public way suggests that they were hardly silent in church, and that they were important enough to the congregation for their

---

[5]For more on Junia, see Eldon Jay Epp, *Junia: The First Woman Apostle* (Minneapolis: Augsburg Fortress, 2005).

[6]One very good summary of these women can be found in Margaret Y. MacDonald, "Reading Real Women through the Undisputed Letters of Paul," in *Women & Christian Origins,* ed. Ross Shepard Kraemer and Mary Rose D'Angelo (Oxford: Oxford University Press, 1999).

disagreement to be consequential. In Philemon, Paul greeted Apphia, whom he called his "sister." "Sister" might have been a way to talk about Christian kinship, but it was also sometimes used as a word to describe a woman who was leading a missionary effort.[7] Returning to Romans 16, seven other women are mentioned besides the three we've already met (Phoebe, Prisca, and Junia)—including a woman named Mary who "has worked very hard among you" (16:6). Tryphaena and Tryphosa are also both "workers in the Lord" (16:12). In the same verse we meet Persis, who is "beloved" and "who has worked hard in the Lord." In addition, the mother of Rufus—whose name Paul may not know, since he does not give it—is "a mother to me also," according to Paul (16:13). Two women, one named Julia and another unnamed (the sister of Nereus) are mentioned in 16:15. Margaret Y. MacDonald has pointed out that Romans 16 "is full of verbs that speak of risk and labor," and that Paul is singling out these women for their bravery and hard work on behalf of the church.[8] These women were the backbone of the churches in Rome and beyond. Even from across the sea, Paul had heard of their hard work and sacrifice.

There Is No Longer Male and Female

This is what I mean when I suggest that we trust Paul's actions as evidence of his commitments. The average person reading Paul will come away with mixed messages, some of which sound very misogynistic to people today. There are passages from Paul's letters—and letters and sections of letters falsely attributed to Paul—that can be difficult to understand, and even to reconcile with each other. First Corinthians 7 and 11 seem to offer visions of women praying and prophesying in church and participating as equal partners in marriage, but just a few chapters later, in 1 Corinthians 14, we get a very different picture. In Ephesians and Colossians, two letters Paul probably did not write, we see very strong limits put on women's roles in relationships and in churches. These passages have led to a long history of Christian misogyny, most of which has been built on a foundation laid by Paul or pseudo-Pauls writing in his name. When I arrived on my college campus as a freshman, the reasons I was surprised to encounter a woman as campus minister were mostly rooted in readings of Paul. When Rev. Dempsey was let go from her position some years later, it was very likely at least partly the result of these very passages from Paul and from writings attributed to him. Christianity has a long history of silencing women in family, church, and society, and most of the time

[7]Ibid., 206.
[8]Ibid., 207.

Paul is a major part of the rationale. But as I hope I've shown, these harmful and misogynistic behaviors and beliefs are mostly not due to Paul himself. They come from misinterpretations of Paul, and they come from writings that were added later to Paul's letters, or from letters that claim to have been written by Paul but weren't. Later Christians, writing in Paul's name and badly interpreting Paul's writings, created Paul the misogynist as we know him today.

By reading between the lines of Paul's writings, in places such as Romans 16 we can see something of how Paul acted in the world. What we see there is that he deeply valued and praised women such as Phoebe, Prisca, Junia, and the other women of Romans 16. He spoke about them as deacons and apostles, as hard workers and risk-takers and colleagues. He *assumed* that women were allowed to do this work, because he *knew* women *were* doing this work, often to his own benefit and on his behalf. These between-the-lines readings help us to make sense of passages such as 1 Corinthians 7:2–7, where Paul describes marriage in egalitarian terms, and 1 Corinthians 11:2–16, where he *assumes* that women are praying and prophesying in church. Such readings also help us to understand what Paul means in Galatians 3:28 when he says that "there is no longer male and female, for all of you are one in Christ Jesus." Paul was no misogynist, no matter how much later Christians tried to make him into one to serve their own misogynistic purposes. Paul understood that something new was happening—that "all of you are one in Christ Jesus"—women just as much as men.

None of this erases Christianity's long history of misogyny, abuse, and denial of women's callings. This chapter has been about how Paul has been unfairly used by the church as a weapon against women, but the truth is that the church itself has perpetrated immense amounts of harm, with or without Paul. The church has erased women's work, silenced their voices, and demonized them in various ways. Paul was an unwilling accomplice in these acts, but this does that mean that the church itself is innocent.

At a minimum, the church has years (perhaps centuries) of work to do on two fronts. First, it has to acknowledge and atone for the harm it has caused in the past. Misogynistic theologies do not simply disappear once we start ordaining women, and our history follows us everywhere we go. For generations to come, the church will need to reckon with its legacy of hurt and harm toward women. This is a prerequisite for any future the church can hope to have. Second, the church must pledge to include *fully*. Persons of all genders are gifted and called by God, and the church must work to honor and respond to the gifts and calls of all people. Paul recognized this when he lifted up the apostolic work of

Junia, the diaconal service of Phoebe, and the leadership of the other women he counted on and praised. But thinking of Paul as an ally is only a *starting point* for the hard work the church has ahead of it. "There is no longer male and female," the apostle could claim, but in the structures, hierarchies, theologies, and liturgies of the church, there still is male and female, justice bifurcated along the artificial lines of gender. To grow into what God is calling us to be, the church has to undo the injustice of the past and live into the justice of the future.

CHAPTER 3

Paul the Homophobe

Candace and Stephanie

My first job after graduating from seminary was at a picturesque and friendly church in the mountains of Asheville, North Carolina. I was only twenty-four years old and not at all sure that I wanted to be in ministry, but Biltmore United Methodist Church welcomed me and nurtured me in the way that really good churches do. Asheville is known as a progressive island in an area that is otherwise moderate-to-conservative, and the church fit that description pretty well too. It was an interesting mixture of people, with a variety of beliefs and approaches to religion. One of my first tasks after taking the job was teaching a year-long Bible study, and it was that experience and others like it that eventually led me to pursue a Ph.D. in biblical interpretation and become a professor of history and New Testament. A lot of what I love about teaching had its beginning in the upstairs classroom where we met every Wednesday night.

There was a woman in that first class named Candace. I could tell that Candace was a little nervous about being there, but also very, very focused on the class. She was a young professional, about my age, who had moved to town from a neighboring state. Candace was a vocal participant in the class, but there was always an edge in her voice that said that there was something *important* at stake for her in our conversations. For her, our Bible study wasn't merely academic, and it wasn't something she was doing just to get out of the house on a weeknight. Candace spoke and participated like someone whose life was on the line. Even in the most obscure parts of the biblical text, she had insightful questions about how to interpret what it said, and she was rarely satisfied with easy answers.

As time passed and I got to know Candace better, it became clear to me *why* she had such an intense and personal stake in the biblical text. Candace was in a relationship with a woman named Stephanie. They weren't "out" yet, at least not at the church, but they lived together and attended the church together, and it wasn't hard to see what was going on. As a young woman who came from a conservative Christian background, Candace was rapidly coming to terms with her own sexuality and identity, and a big part of that was happening in our Bible study. All the questions she had about the biblical text came out of her own experiences. The intensity she brought to our discussions flowed out of her religious upbringing, which had taught her that the very thing she was beginning to understand about herself—that she was gay—was unholy, sinful, and wrong. But Candace knew better, and she had signed up for the Bible study as a way to understand her spirituality and reconcile it with her whole self, including her sexuality.

As time went on, I learned that Candace's relationship with her mother was going through a rough patch. She didn't say why, but of course I had my suspicions. After a few months, I sent Candace an email, asking whether she wanted to talk about her relationships with Stephanie and with her mother, and hinting that the two might be connected. It was like a dam had broken; she was eager to talk about it, and Candace, Stephanie, and I got together over dinner one night before the Bible study. We talked about how difficult it was to be lesbian, even in a progressive city and church, and how Candace's mother was having a hard time accepting her daughter's sexuality. We talked about Christianity, whether Stephanie and Candace saw any place for themselves in the church, and whether the church would ever be able to accept them for who they are. (The United Methodist Church was divided over the issue of human sexuality then, in the early 2000s, and it remains deeply divided today.) And, we talked about the Bible, especially the so-called "clobber texts" that are always quoted in debates about homosexuality. As with most gay and lesbian Christians (and former Christians) I've met since, Candace knew them by heart: Genesis 1:27; Genesis 19; Leviticus 18:22; Leviticus 20:13; Deuteronomy 23:17–18; Romans 1:26–27; 1 Corinthians 6:9–10; 1 Timothy 1:9–11; and Jude 1:7. Some of these passages are used more commonly than others, and some are more clearly relevant to the question of homosexuality than others, but these are the texts that people such as Candace have usually had thrown in their faces. These verses are the source of uncertainty, pain, and isolation for millions of gay and lesbian Christians. In the hands of Christians, these passages have destroyed lives. And, as you probably have noticed, *three* of them come with Paul's name attached to them.

Clobber Texts

For people such as Candace, the Bible can feel like an enemy, and Paul can feel like the biggest threat of all because he's listed as the author of three of the "clobber texts," the passages used to dehumanize and condemn people who are gay and lesbian. In Romans 1:26–27, 1 Corinthians 6:9–10, and 1 Timothy 1:9–11, the biblical authors are describing actions that are anathema to God: theft, drunkenness, murder, slave trading, dishonesty, and all sorts of other terrible things. Included in these lists—and especially prominent in the Romans passage—are sexual practices such as prostitution and fornication, and "shameless acts" of "sodomy" and "unnatural" kinds of sex, which are often translated and interpreted as homosexuality or same-sex acts. It's a harrowing list to read if you're gay and trying to be a faithful Christian. It's terrifying to see yourself there among slave traders, thieves, and murderers of parents. Many faithful people have been battered and assaulted by these "clobber texts" until they have left the church or stopped believing in God altogether. The damage done by these passages, wielded by Christians and authorized by Paul's name, is incalculable.

The people who cite and wield these texts seem to think that their meaning is very clear. They have a lot of confidence about what a "sodomite" is, and what counts as "natural" and "unnatural" intercourse, even though Paul doesn't stop to explain these things in any detail. Such people easily equate the things Paul is describing with modern relationships, as if 20 centuries and vastly different cultures didn't stand between us and Paul's words. They rely on Paul's words as they are presented in English translations, even though such persons seldom have much sense of what the Greek says, what nuances might be masked in the translation, or the ways in which the translations themselves might be carrying ideological weight. They treat these verses in isolation, as if they weren't part of much larger books with larger agendas, and they treat the Bible itself as an uncomplicated handbook for life, which it definitely is not (and is not trying to be). The folks who go around clobbering gay and lesbian people with these "clobber texts" see a lot of clarity in them, but these texts are anything but clear. Like all ancient texts, these require careful reading and interpretation, and we have to resist the temptation to fill them up with our own biases and expectations. After all, Paul never met my friends Candace and Stephanie, and when we read his words as if he were talking about them, we do violence to Paul's words. More importantly, we do violence to Candace and Stephanie, harming them in Paul's name.

All three of these passages are examples of what scholars call "vice lists." Paul used these lists a lot in his writing, and pseudo-Pauline writers (such as the author of 1 Timothy) used them too, to make their writing look more like Paul's. Vice lists (and virtue lists) had a long history before Paul, and Paul used them to summarize briefly and succinctly the kinds of ethics and behavior that he thought were bad (or good). Most often, Paul used them to describe the behaviors that he thought were characteristic of gentiles; like most Jews of the day, Paul held stereotypical views about gentiles.[1]

The most famous vice and virtue lists in the New Testament are found in Galatians 5, in which Paul lists the "works of the flesh" in 5:19–21 and the "fruits of the spirit" in 5:22–23. In those lists, Paul is clearly contrasting the kinds of behaviors he thinks people will exhibit when they "live by the Spirit" with the kinds of behaviors the "flesh" produces. Paul doesn't mention same-sex behavior in Galatians, but he does mention another sexual activity—fornication—that appears frequently in the New Testament, including in both 1 Corinthians 6:9 and 1 Timothy 1:10.

Bible scholars debate whether Paul was coming up with these vice and virtue lists each time, or simply repeating a stock list that he might have gotten somewhere else.[2] I think it likely that he was working from stock lists and not making up a new one each time, since the lists he produced are quite similar to one another. But Paul's lists do seem to be tailored to his own specific concerns, because they focus on two major things: general morality and idolatry. By general morality, I mean that Paul thinks it's bad to kill, steal, lie, cheat, and so on. These are general bad-behavior categories that wouldn't have been particular to Judaism or the Jesus movement, but broadly applicable to everyone. Nobody (or almost nobody) thought it was ethically proper do those things. But the second category, idolatry, is where Paul seems to have adapted standard vice lists to fit his own purposes. Some of the sexual activities Paul mentions in these lists, such as prostitution and same-sex acts, have as much to do with idolatry as they do with sexual pleasure. We'll look closely at some of these idolatrous sexual activities in a few pages, but for now we should stop to notice that all three of Paul's "clobber texts" that people use to condemn homosexuality come within one of these lists. The passage

---

[1]My colleague Pamela Eisenbaum has a great discussion of these Jewish attitudes toward gentiles, if you want to know more about them. See Pamela Eisenbaum, *Paul Was Not a Christian: The Original Message of a Misunderstood Apostle* (New York: HarperOne, 2009), 152–53.

[2]James R. Harrison, "Virtues and Vices: New Testament Ethical Exhortation in Its Graeco-Roman Context," *Oxford Bibliographies* (Oxford University Press, May 24, 2017), DOI: 10.1093/OBO/9780195393361-0236.

from Romans fits this category least well, but even the Romans passage is essentially a vice list in narrative form. To put it differently: nowhere does Paul simply launch into a discussion of homosexuality; his comments are always deeply embedded in material he has taken from somewhere else, and very much concerned with what Paul sees as the stereotypically idolatrous acts of gentiles. Paul never thinks about same-sex sexual activity on its own—certainly not in the way our twenty-first–century society does—but always as part of a larger pattern of things he thinks gentiles do. These "clobber texts" about homosexuality aren't even about homosexuality, *really*. They're about Paul's understanding of gentiles and what they need to change about their ethics if they are to reflect their new status as people who "live by the Spirit."

Not only are these passages not really about homosexuality in any specific way, but there is a huge debate among scholars about what Paul was even talking about. Modern translations often use words such as "sodomites" and "homosexuals" in these passages, but those translations wildly overstate the words Paul actually used, which are much more vague and general. People who throw these texts in the faces of gay and lesbian people today usually miss the fact that these so-called "clobber texts" are actually more about idolatry than sex, and they therefore distort Paul's meaning. And, in the case of one of these passages, the people quoting it usually don't acknowledge that Paul likely didn't even write it. In short, the way these "clobber texts" have been used is a kind of scriptural malpractice, misunderstanding them at nearly every opportunity. This malpractice has had dire consequences for millions of lives. In the next few sections, we will look at the three "clobber texts" associated with Paul—Romans 1:26–27; 1 Corinthians 6:9–10; and 1 Timothy 1:9–11—and see just how much modern prejudice and misunderstanding has been packed into these few short verses.

Pseudo-Paul's Clobber Text

First Timothy 1:9–11 is a very standard vice list, the kind used by many different people in the ancient world, and especially by Paul. Paul was fond of rattling off these lists of bad behaviors as a way to summarize how the root problem of idolatry had compromised the morality and ethics of gentiles. It's not surprising that we would find this kind of list in a book that has Paul's name on it; this kind of vice list is very characteristic of Paul's writing, and it fits right in with his style and the themes of his work. Lists of bad things that gentiles do is *very Paul*.

As we saw in the first chapter, though, there's one problem with this. While this vice list from 1 Timothy is very typical of Paul's writing, 1

Timothy itself is probably *not* Paul's writing. First Timothy is one of the pastoral epistles, along with 2 Timothy and Titus. These books claim to be written by Paul, and they even contain the kinds of biographical and literary details that make them seem plausible as authentic letters from Paul. But most scholars, particularly those without strong conservative religious ties, see the pastoral epistles as pseudo-Pauline compositions—"forgeries," to use the language of one prominent Bible scholar.[3] These books, including 1 Timothy, were likely written long after Paul's death, by people who wanted to influence Paul's legacy and the communities he left behind. I particularly like Margaret M. Mitchell's way of putting it: these books were written "to 'fix' his legacy (in both senses of the term)"—to solidify Paul's authority, but also to capitalize on that same authority to correct what the pseudo-Paul authors thought of as deficiencies or gaps in Paul's authentic writings.[4] This includes "fixing" Paul's teachings about women's roles, as we saw in the last chapter, but also providing more input on things such as church governance, which would not have been as much of a concern in Paul's own day.

The vice list found in 1 Timothy 1:9–11 is mostly a "fix" for Paul's legacy in the sense that it helps solidify that legacy in place, not in the sense that it corrects it. This is a reiteration of material from Paul's undisputed letters, not an addition to it. But the very act of reiteration—repeating something from Paul's other letters—also amounts to a "fix" of the other kind. By choosing particular aspects of Paul's writing to lift out and repeat, the author of 1 Timothy was placing an emphasis on those parts of Paul's writings, and not others. It's no accident that 1 Timothy features this vice list very early in the letter. It is a way of condemning "certain people" who were teaching a tradition different from the one that the author of the letter was teaching. The author of 1 Timothy was very keen to establish up front from just what kind of depravity that opponent's perspective came. The "fix" here is to restate Paul's condemnation of licentious and sinful gentile morality.

Among the vices the author lists in these verses is a peculiar and controversial one. In verse 10, sandwiched between fornicators and slave traders, is the Greek word *arsenokoites* (plural *arsenokoitai*). Fewer words in the New Testament have inspired more debate, perhaps because the word itself is not very well known outside of the New Testament and related writings. This word has been translated into English in a variety of different ways, reflecting the difficulty of understanding

---

[3]Bart D. Ehrman, *Forged: Writing in the Name of God—Why the Bible's Authors Are Not Who We Think They Are* (San Francisco: Harper Collins, 2011).

[4]Margaret M. Mitchell, Introduction to the Pastoral Epistles in *New Oxford Annotated Bible (NRSV with Apocrypha)*, 5th Edition (Oxford: Oxford University Press, 2018).

exactly what it means: "sodomites" (NRSV and RSV), "those practicing homosexuality" (NIV), "men who practice homosexuality" (ESV), "people who have intercourse with the same sex" (CEB), "them that defile themselves with mankind" (KJV), "homosexuals" (NASB and many others), "those who do sex sins with their own sex" (NLV), and "sexual perverts" (*Good News*). At least one scholarly commentary suggests "pederasts" as the best translation,[5] while other scholarship notes that "its [the word's] connotation is economic," meaning that it might refer specifically to sex work.[6]

These different translations reflect the fact that the word itself is a compound word, created from the Greek words for "bed" and "man." What the relationship is between those words is less clear. Is this referring to someone who "beds" men as a matter of preference, or as a matter of economic necessity, or because they had no choice because of their social status? (See the section below on Romans 1:26–27 for more on this last possibility.) The different translations listed above try to make sense of the word, but, in doing so, the biases of the translators show through. The generic "homosexuals" is a blanket term that assumes that the author of 1 Timothy meant to condemn the large group of people who are attracted to, and have sex with, people of the same sex—including women. Some are more specific and mention "men who practice homosexuality." Perhaps the worst translation of all is found in the RSV and the NRSV, which use "sodomites." The Greek word *arsenokoites* has nothing to do with Sodom, etymologically or historically—and, besides, the "sin of Sodom" was inhospitality, not a certain kind of sexuality. Besides, "sodomy" can refer to a wide variety of sexual activities that can't or don't lead to procreation, all of which are practiced by representatives of all sexual orientations.

No matter what translation we choose, it will inevitably be inadequate. All translations are approximations, and in the case of a word such as this one, we simply don't know enough about the ancient meaning to put it into English confidently. It does seem clear that the author of 1 Timothy meant to imply some kind of sexual transgression, and the combination of "man" and "bed" probably means that the word refers to sexual activity between two men. What kind of activity the author had in mind remains unclear, but its inclusion in this vice list does mean that the author of 1 Timothy likely disapproved

---

[5] "Same-Sex Relations," in *The Oxford Encyclopedia of the Bible and Gender Studies*, ed. David Tabb Stewart, Thomas K. Hubbard, Anthony Corbeill, Lynn R. Huber, David Brodsky, and Valerie Abrahamsen. Oxford Biblical Studies Online, http://www.oxfordbiblicalstudies.com/article/opr/t453/e40 (accessed Aug. 30, 2018).

[6] Martin Dibelius and Hans Conzelmann, *The Pastoral Epistles*, Hermeneia—A Critical and Historical Commentary on the Bible (Minneapolis: Fortress Press, 1989).

of some kind of sex between men. This isn't surprising, considering the context. The author, after all, was using the vice list to express a very stereotypically Jewish attitude toward gentiles, and there is lots of evidence that Jewish stereotypes of gentiles in that period included condemnations of homosexuality.[7] Looking at 1 Timothy, the best thing I can say in defense of Paul is that he didn't write this book. He did, however, inspire someone to write it, and the inclusion of *arsenokoites* in this vice list from 1 Timothy probably came from imitating one of Paul's authentic letters, 1 Corinthians. In that letter, in another vice list, Paul used *arsenokoites*, and another strange word, *malakos*. Let's look at that passage now.

Malakoi and Arsenokoitai

Unlike 1 Timothy, there is little doubt that Paul wrote 1 Corinthians. After Romans, 1 Corinthians might be Paul's best-known letter, and together with 2 Corinthians it represents the most vivid back-and-forth between Paul and one of his communities that has survived to the present. It is clear that the Corinthians and Paul cared deeply about each other—deeply enough to argue, criticize each other, share joys and sorrows, and be in relationship across a number of years, in person and apart. This letter contains lots of Paul's anger, frustration, and pain, all coming from his interactions with the Corinthians, but it also shows his tenderness toward them as his beloved congregation. This combination of Paul's disapproval of the Corinthians' behavior with his pastoral exhortations to them leads him, in chapter 6, to use a vice list. As he does in other places in his letters, he uses this vice list to suggest the kinds of behaviors typical of gentiles but unbecoming for someone who hopes to "inherit the kingdom of God"(6:9).

This vice list is roughly organized with sexual vices listed first and more generic ones listed last, although as always all these seem to flow out of the experience of idolatry. Paul's list of people guilty of sexual vices in 1 Corinthians 6:9–10 includes fornicators (a mainstay of these lists), adulterers, and two categories of people that have bearing on the question of this chapter—which is whether or not Paul was a homophobe. The second of these categories is familiar from the last section: *arsenokoitai*. In fact, this section of 1 Corinthians might well be where the pseudonymous author of 1 Timothy found the word, and from where he decided to "borrow" it to use as a conspicuously

---

[7]The annotations of 1 Timothy in the *Jewish Annotated New Testament,* which were written by Naomi Koltun-Fromm, point to several Jewish writers who expressed this kind of condemnation, including Philo, Josephus, and Pseudo-Phocylides). Naomi Koltun-Fromm, "The First Letter of Paul to Timothy," in *The Jewish Annotated New Testament,* 2d ed. (Oxford: Oxford University Press, 2017), 433.

"Paul-ish" word—to lend credence to his imitation of Paul's style. The first category, though, uses a word that we haven't seen yet, and it's another one that's very controversial and difficult to translate: *malakos*. Paul lists *malakoi* (which is the plural) among the kinds of people who cannot hope to inherit the kingdom of God, alongside thieves and drunkards. Just as with *arsenokoites*, different translations do different things with this word: "effeminate" (KJV, ASV, NASB) is relatively literal, while "passive homosexual partners" (NET) ties the word to specific sexual practice, and even a specific role within that practice. The CEB reads *arsenokoitai* and *malakoi* together, and translates them "both participants in same-sex intercourse," with an alternate option of "submissive and dominant male sexual partners" in the notes (something similar to what the ESV does). Other translations, such as the NIV, also translate the words together as "men who have sex with men." The RSV translated them together as "sexual perverts." Even at a surface level, you can see the homophobic ideology of the translators at work in some of these editions.

The confusion comes from the fact that *malakos* is a Greek word that means "soft," but it sometimes takes on specific secondary meanings having to do with being the receiving partner in a relationship between two men, or, alarmingly, between a man and a boy. There is a huge range of possibly meanings here, from a man who is not stereotypically masculine (a man who is "soft") to a boy who is a victim of an older man. Many translations understand this word to be part of a pair with *arsenokoitai*, and assume that they are describing the two roles in a sexual encounter between two men. In Paul's vice lists, he does tend to group words together that he thinks of as having something in common, so perhaps Paul did intend to describe two roles in a relationship between men. But we can't discount the possibility that Paul was intending to describe an abusive situation in which an adult man was having sex with a boy, or an adult man of a higher status was having sex with a man of a lower status. This latter possibility, in fact, is a strong possibility for interpreting Romans 1:26–27, to which we turn in the next section.

While there are several interpretations of 1 Corinthians 6:9–10 that point in other directions, let's assume for a moment that Paul *did* mean this passage to condemn relationships between adult men. (There is no hint of relationships between women in this passage.) What should we do with this passage then? Is a passage such as this enough for modern Christians to condemn men who are in homosexual relationships? Should this passage give Christians license to exclude or marginalize gay men today? The answer is no. There are at least three major reasons why. I'll talk about them only briefly here, because I'm going to revisit them all at the end of the chapter.

First, we have to remember what we are reading here. First Corinthians is a *letter*. It is someone else's mail. It was never meant for us; Paul wrote it for an audience of Greek Christians in the early 50s C.E., and he had in mind the particular concerns of that community. He never imagined that anyone like us would be reading this letter, dozens of lifetimes later in lands he never knew. If he had known about us, he might have written it differently. When Paul wrote those two Greek words in 1 Corinthians 6:9–10, he wasn't worried about whether *we* would understand them. He knew his Greek-speaking audience in Corinth would understand them, with all their nuance and local meaning. We have no way of knowing the particular circumstances that led him to include these two words in his vice list in the middle of his letter—what social or cultural conflicts had provoked him, what religious biases might have motivated him, what specific persons in the Corinthian congregation he might have had in mind. Paul was not trying to set sexual ethics for the next twenty centuries in this letter. He was simply trying to respond to life in Corinth and motivate the people there to live in certain kinds of ways. We don't know everything about his reasons for saying what he said, but we do know that by the time his words reach us today, they have traveled a long, long way from their starting point.

Second, there is no reason to think that Paul understood the vices described in 1 Corinthians 6:9–10 in any way that was different from any other vice he talks about in the letter. In the same sentence, Paul names others who "will not inherit the kingdom of God." He says that "fornicators" will not inherit the kingdom of God; well, approximately *95 percent* of Americans have sex before marriage.[8] In the way Paul wrote this sentence, there is absolute equivalency between those 95 percent and *malakoi* and *arsenokoitai*. Thieves, Paul writes, will not inherit the kingdom of God. Have you ever stolen anything, even a pen from work? The greedy will not inherit the kingdom of God either, Paul says, but he doesn't qualify what greedy means. Did you buy this book from an online retailer to save a few bucks? Does that count? Or, did you take an extra slice of pie at Thanksgiving last year? What about the "drunkards" that Paul includes on that list? Ever had one too many drinks? No kingdom of God for you!

Paul doesn't make distinctions between the vices on his list, and he doesn't distinguish between gradations of those vices, either. Modern

[8]Lawrence B. Finer, "Trends in Premarital Sex in the United States, 1954–2003," *Public Health Reports* 122, no. 1 (2007): 73–78.

Christians are the ones who have decided that the "sodomites" and "practicing homosexuals" in our modern translations deserve special condemnation, but in making that judgment they are reading things into Paul's writing that just aren't there. That special bias belongs to people today, not to Paul, and the fact that we dwell on it so intensely says more about us than it does about him.

Finally, when we are reading passages such as 1 Corinthians 6:9–10, we do well to remember that we live in a profoundly different culture and society than Paul did. I will return to this point in a few pages, so I won't belabor it now. Suffice it to say that Paul, in the first-century Mediterranean world, did not possess all the same cognitive categories that we do. He didn't see the world as we see it. For Paul, men having sex with men didn't fit in any of his categories or ways of thinking about the world or human interaction. He didn't have a way to think about two men (or two women) in a mutually committed, loving relationship. He didn't have any way to think about people who don't conform to strict standards of masculinity or femininity (except to call some men "soft"). He didn't know what to do with sex outside of marriage—which, in *our* world, is breathtakingly common—except to call it "fornication." In short, Paul had no cognitive category for homosexuality, or for most of the ways we think about sex today generally. (More on this in chapter 5.) Paul likely never met anyone similar to my friends Candace and Stephanie, who now own a house together, have children together, go to church together, and share love, care, affection, and grace with one another. They don't look anything like what Paul describes in 1 Corinthians, and, as we will see in the next section, they don't look anything like what Paul describes in Romans, either.

Paul and Passion

This passage from Romans (1:26–27) is the clearest and strongest statement Paul makes against same-sex activities, so I've saved it for last. Unlike 1 Timothy, Paul definitely wrote Romans—no serious scholar disputes that. And, unlike 1 Corinthians 6:9–10, there's little confusion about what Paul meant to say in this passage, and no suspicious translation trickery—although, as with any translation, there are things that are made less clear by putting it into English. This passage from Romans is definitely Paul, and it's reasonably clear what he meant by it, and so this has long been a favorite text for people who claim that Paul opposed homosexuality—and that the Bible and God oppose it, by extension. Here is Paul the homophobe at his most homophobic, it would seem. What are we to make of this passage? Is this proof that homosexuality is sinful, and that Paul was writing this passage so that everyone would know it?

I don't think this passage is proof of any such thing. Far from proving that homosexuality is a sin and that God opposes it, I see these two verses from Romans as proving something different: that Paul was a very normal first-century person and a very typical Jewish person, who was skeptical about idolatry, opposed to oppression, and interested in upholding his own community's perspective on sexuality against what he thought of as gentile indecency. Furthermore, when Paul was writing these verses, I don't think he was thinking about sin and sinfulness at all; he was instead thinking about what was "natural" and proper, and he was thinking about the ways society can be organized around and predicated on injustice and abuse. This is not to say that Paul did or would have supported same-sex activities or relationships in the modern sense. It's clear that he opposed the former, and, as we've seen, he didn't have the conceptual framework to think about the latter. But it's important to try to understand *why* Paul wrote the things he wrote, and once we start to look closely at things in this way, a very different picture emerges about what Paul could have meant by this passage.

Let's start with the context of these two verses—because, after all, they are a part of a much longer letter. Verses 26 and 27 come as part of an introduction to his letter to the Romans, just after Paul has sent greetings and said a bit about why he is writing. Beginning in 1:16, Paul launches into a long rationale for the letter, but also for his ministry. It's clear from the beginning of this section that Paul is talking about gentiles, and about the state of moral and religious degradation he imagines them to be in. This whole section takes the form of a narrativized vice list, and in fact it ends with a *proper* vice list in some of the last verses of the chapter, in 29–31. Throughout this section, Paul is setting out why he is writing to the churches in Rome, and by extension why he wants to visit the Roman churches as part of his missionary journeys westward. It's because he thinks that gentiles are living in a state of ignorance and unholiness, reveling in what is unnatural and unaware of the truth of God. It's Paul's job, he thinks, to bring light to the nations, make them aware of the saving work of Jesus, and bring them into the fold in the last days before God decisively intervenes in history. It makes sense that he would begin by laying out the problem: gentiles are almost hopelessly lost, morally confused, and foolish. Once he has stated the problem, he is free to spend most of the rest of the letter laying out the solution, which Paul firmly believed was to be found in the life, death, and resurrection of Jesus.

We can see Paul stating the problem by looking at the language he uses in verses 26 and 27. He talks about "degrading passions," which led to "unnatural" intercourse for women and men committing "shameless acts" with each other. These are the kinds of words and phrases that might *seem to us* to have plain meanings, but that really contain complicated stories and lots of cultural baggage. Once we start to unpack that baggage and understand the stories these verses are telling, we can see that the meaning of these verses isn't as plain as some people claim.

"Passion" is one of those words that might seem to have a plain meaning, but doesn't. The Greek here is *pathos,* and like most words in most languages, it had a range of meanings; but the one that probably fits best here is "a passive state" or "a condition."[9] When Paul uses "passion," he isn't talking about lust, exactly—at least not in any simple or specific sense. Rather, he's talking about a weakness or helplessness that comes over you, or something that you're overcome by. This is why that whole sentence places human beings ("them") in the passive position. *"God gave them up"* (emphasis author's), abandoning them to be overcome by that which they could not control, because—as Paul had said earlier in verse 24—of idolatry. The same-sex activities described in 26 and 27 are the *effects,* not the cause. The root cause was idolatry, and, because of that idolatry, Paul says God saw fit to give humans over to the overwhelming passions that come with being human.

The end result of this, Paul says, is that men engage in sex with men, and women with women, because they can't help it. It just comes over them, and they have to give in. But I repeat: this is an *effect* of sin, not a *cause* of it, and for Paul the really important issue is the idolatry that started the whole thing. This effect of gentile idolatry is not itself sinful, but *is,* Paul thinks, unnatural. I see a hole in Paul's logic here, because the way I read this passage is that God gave them up to do what they were *naturally* inclined to do anyway, but the end result is the same. To Paul, women having sex with women and men having sex with men was unnatural.

It's not hard to see what he means here, and it's all rooted in the ideas Paul had about the purpose of sex. To him, sex was for procreation. This was an extremely common understanding of sex in those days (and our own day), and for both Paul and for many people today it's an understanding of sex that's rooted in the Bible. In Genesis, after all, humans are commanded to go forth and multiply, and sex is the

[9]H.G. Liddell and Robert Scott, *An Intermediate Greek-English Lexicon* (Oxford: Clarendon Press, 1889), 584.

way that happens. The *naturalness* of heterosexual sex must have been obvious to Paul, and to most other Jewish and Christian people of the day. For his time, Paul had a very normal and uncomplicated idea of heterosexual sex—the kind that leads to procreation—as "natural," and anything else as "unnatural." Paul looked at gentiles, whom he stereotyped as sexually promiscuous, and he said, "Aha! This is what comes of all that gentile idolatry!"

Of course, today we have a very different understanding of what's "natural" about sex. We know that sex is usually about more than reproduction, and that even people who don't want to or can't procreate have sex that would be quite "natural" by Paul's own standard. We also organize our knowledge about sex and sexuality very differently from Paul; we don't assume that a man who enjoys and desires sex with women will suddenly, after engaging in religious idolatry, start having sex with men, or vice versa. We understand sex in our twenty-first–century ways, which are very different from Paul's first-century ways, and much more informed by science. The premise of Paul's argument, which is that our sexuality can be changed simply by God "giving us up," doesn't work for us today. Furthermore, we know plenty of gay and lesbian people who procreate, so clearly the dichotomies from Paul's day don't hold true for us today. What counted as "natural" in the first century doesn't make much sense for us in the twenty-first century.

But there is one major idea upon which I think progressive Christians can agree with Paul in Romans 1:26–27 (and in 1 Corinthians 6:9–10, from the previous section). It's the ethical principle behind a lot of what he says about homosexuality: Paul, in Romans, wants to protect people from exploitation and abuse. While we tend to think that sex, whether heterosexual or homosexual, as something that ought to occur between consenting adult individuals, that was not always or even usually the case in Paul's days. The Roman world in which Paul lived was very stratified, with some people occupying privileged positions and others having nearly no personal agency or identity. Very often, sex was the means by which that hierarchy was announced and enforced. Everyone, from one end of the social order to the other, lived in a web of relationships defined by honor, shame, duty, obligation, dominance, and submission. A slaveholder, for instance, had near absolute power and authority over the people he enslaved, and one important means to signal that power and authority was the sexual penetration of the subordinate by the dominant—both women and men. It was shameful for the slaveholder to be penetrated by the enslaved, but the opposite was permitted and even considered proper. Even among free persons,

sexual penetration of one man by another could be used to show the
social dominance in the relationship.[10] In the Roman world, being
penetrated was an effeminate posture, and penetrating was a masculine
posture. In the twenty-first century we understand that such simple
dichotomies are unhelpful, and in any case deeply misogynistic. But
in the first century they were the conventional wisdom of the world.
When Paul speaks disapprovingly about men having sex with men, it's
partly because he understands that those kinds of sexual relationships
are often or usually exploitative and nonconsensual. They were the
evidence of a human passion—helplessness—that flowed out of idolatry.
Whatever else we think about the reasoning behind it, the impulse to
limit abuse is a good one, and Paul doubtless strongly condemned this
system of sexual exploitation. Unfortunately, as have so many people
today, he also confused abuse with healthy expressions of sexuality,
lumping them all together and condemning them all.

Paul, an Ally for LGBTQI Justice

I have spent a lot of this chapter defending Paul. I have claimed,
in essence, that Paul's words are not as harsh and condemning as they
appear to be. I have pointed out that Paul lived in a very different time
and place, during which there were different understandings of human
sexuality and different social patterns that led Paul to say the things he
said. I have argued that Paul was not the author of 1 Timothy, and that
the actual author of that letter was likely trying to "fix" Paul's legacy by
imitating Paul's language to enforce social norms in his own day. Paul's
comments in 1 Corinthians, meanwhile, use the vague and confusing
terms *malakoi* and *arsenokoitai,* which have given rise to some especially
homophobic modern translations—but this passage also reminds
us that Paul lacked the categories to think about homosexual sex as
a mutual and consensual activity. The verses from Romans are Paul's
strongest and clearest condemnation of same-sex love, but even there
his language is unclear, and Paul's words are probably influenced by his
desire to condemn exploitative and abusive forms of sex. After all, Paul
didn't live in the same world we do, and the relationships he thought
of as normative don't look very much like the ones we know today. In
all, I've pointed out how Paul's comments about homosexuality always
come in vice lists: standard lists of misdeeds that Paul likely borrowed

---

[10]In this section I am mostly following the work of Robert Jewett, whose
Romans commentary includes a helpful section on this material, including a
quotation from Seneca, a prominent Roman author from antiquity, which helps
to illustrate the ubiquity of sex as a social marker: "Sexual servicing is a crime for
the freeborn, a necessity for a slave, and a duty for the freeman." Robert Jewett,
Romans: A Commentary, Hermeneia–A Critical and Historical Commentary on the
Bible (Minneapolis: Fortress, 2007), 180–81.

from common usage. Because this is where the words *malakoi* and *arsenokoitai* appear, we have to be careful not to read too much into Paul's use of them. If he was simply repeating stock phrases, as seems likely, then Paul wasn't meaning to single out gay and lesbian people any more than he was meaning to single out any of the other very common activities on those lists. In reciting those lists, Paul wanted to draw attention to gentile morality, and call gentiles into a more holy—and more Jewish—way of life. The vice lists are expressions of Paul's knee-jerk ethics—an embedded theology of everyday life—and not the kind of thing Paul might have come up with if he had paused to write a holistic ethics.

The fact that we zero in on these three passages from Paul (well, two from Paul and one from pseudo-Paul) is itself troubling—for 1 Corinthians 6:9–10; Romans 1:26–27; and 1 Timothy 1:9–11 are *not* the final word from Paul on sexuality, theology, or ethics. As much as some Christians would like to read them that way, these passages are *not* Paul's definitive and mature reasoning on the matter, and certainly not the Bible's final word. These passages come in the flow of letters written to particular people under particular circumstances, on which we eavesdrop as we read. These vice lists aren't Paul's attempts to say what is most important about God, the world, Jesus, life, or religion. They are part of larger arguments that he's making about Jews and gentiles, the importance of forsaking idolatry, and the new promise of God that is evident in the life and death of Jesus.

This last point is especially important to keep in mind. The whole reason that Paul wrote letters, or engaged in missionary work with communities such as the one in Corinth at all, was that he had become convinced that the life, death, and resurrection of Jesus was a sign. He saw in Jesus the evidence that God was doing a new thing: opening up God's family to gentiles in the last days. Paul understood that he was living at the end of an age—and perhaps at the end of time itself—and that the God of Israel had inaugurated a new era by raising Jesus from the dead. Jesus, for Paul, was the "first fruits of those who have died," the sign that God was overthrowing death and offering salvation to all of humanity (1 Cor. 15:20). In the last days, Paul wanted gentiles to turn away from idolatry and sinfulness, and turn toward the God of Israel, who Paul thought was in fact the God of the whole world.

This was the context in which Paul wrote the verses we've examined in this chapter, but it was also the context for him writing a lot of *other* words—words that can help us understand and use Paul as an ally for justice in LGBTQI concerns. Paul didn't just write lists of vices. Paul also wrote beautiful and moving prose, and some of the most affecting parts of his letters are when he is talking about justice and inclusion.

Although Paul himself would not have advocated for LGBTQI inclusion, because the categories in his worldview simply didn't have room for it, his words about inclusion and justice can guide progressive Christians today as we go about that work. Two examples illustrate this point.

Galatians 3:28, Justice, and Inclusion

The first is a very short but famous passage found in Galatians 3:28, with parallel passages in Romans 10:12, Colossians 3:11, and 1 Corinthians 12:13. The Galatians version says: "There is no longer Jew or Greek, there is no longer slave or free, there is no longer male and female; for all of you are one in Christ Jesus." The Colossians version (written by a pseudo-Paul author) includes other kinds of difference that are swallowed up by affiliation with Jesus: circumcised and uncircumcised, barbarian, and Scythian. Paul (and his imitators) wanted to emphasize how things that set people apart from each other become less important in light of common humanity and relationship to God. Chief among these was the difference between Jews and Greeks (with "Greeks" being another way to say "gentiles"), which is the kind of difference that was most obvious to Paul and his communities. But in choosing these different kinds of difference, Paul (and pseudo-Paul) was often using the differences that were most difficult to imagine overcoming in his day. The Scythian was the epitome of an uncivilized person in the early Christian world, the kind of person who would have been unthinkably different from someone living in Corinth or Rome or Colossae.[11] Male and female, in those days, were considered as being as different as night and day. In choosing these pairs of opposites, Paul was trying to describe the deepest difference he could imagine—and then saying that, because of God's work through Jesus, it didn't matter anymore.

The reason variations of this passage appear again and again in the New Testament might be because, as with vice lists, this was a stock phrase that Paul was borrowing and citing in his writing. Some scholars think that these sayings are part of a very early church baptismal ritual; a version of this would have been said after a person was baptized.[12] If so, then this sentiment belongs at the core of the earliest Christian proclamation: the things that divide us become unimportant to God the moment we join God's family. This is an exemplary principle for Christians considering the question of human sexuality: where God

---

[11]Peter Zaas, "The Letter of Paul to the Colossians," in *The Jewish Annotated New Testament,* 2d ed. (Oxford: Oxford University Press, 2017), 415–16.

[12]Hans Dieter Betz, *Galatians,* Hermeneia (Minneapolis: Fortress Press, 1979), 189–201.

has made us one, we should spend no time finding ways to divide ourselves.

1 Corinthians 11:17—13:13, Justice, and Inclusion

The second example I will use from Paul's writing is much longer, but it is less often appreciated and used by progressive Christians arguing for justice and inclusion. In 1 Corinthians, Paul strings together three distinct sections, like movements in a piece of music. These three are very often cited separately, but much less often seen together as three parts of a larger argument. Beginning in 11:17, Paul builds an argument about the meaning and purpose of community, beginning in shared practice and culminating in a meditation on love.

Paul does this sometimes. His writing can be very elliptical, circling back around to take multiple passes at a single idea. He says something, decides that it's not *quite* right, and in the next paragraph takes another run at it. That's what he's doing in this part of 1 Corinthians; he writes three different movements under the same theme, each one building on the last, until in the exquisite poetry of the so-called "love chapter" he completes the composition. The result is the best, most sustained meditation we have from Paul on the subject of Christian community and ethics. It is much more useful as a guide to justice and inclusion than the vice lists are, and this long section should be a foundation for how we think about Paul as an ally for progressive Christian values.

The first movement begins in 11:17, although it builds on something Paul had been doing in the letter since the beginning of chapter 5—that is, responding with increasing exasperation to situations that had arisen in Corinth: sexual ethics and dilemmas, lawsuits, dietary disputes, and the like. In 11:17–34, he addresses another situation: the celebration of the Lord's supper. It seems that social and economic divisions had interfered with what should have been a holy and communal time; when the Corinthians gathered as a church for the Lord's supper, some were going hungry while others were gorging themselves. It's important to notice that this wasn't a symbolic meal, as are today's eucharist or communion services; this was a full meal, a "potluck," that was also at the same time as the Christian ritual. In the early church, this meal was called the *agape,* after a Greek word for love. It was a meal named, literally, for love. The fact that some were treating it like a Vegas buffet—getting drunk and eating all the food and leaving others hungry—made Paul very angry. "I do not commend you," Paul wrote, "because when you come together it is not for the better but for the worse" (1 Cor. 11:17). This leads Paul to remind his readers of the Last Supper tradition that he had received, and to exhort the Corinthians to unity: in the meal and in their community generally. But Paul wasn't done. Bad behavior at the meal named for love sent Paul on a literary trajectory that would last for two more chapters.

Chapter 12 begins with meditation on spiritual gifts—more things that were dividing the church in Corinth. Some people, it seems, were promoting their gifts as especially important, and members of the community were denigrating each other's gifts as unimportant. Paul's answer to this disunity is his famous metaphor of the body of Christ. The whole community, Paul argues, is like a body—Christ's body. The individual parts of that body cannot then say to the others that they are unimportant; they have to work together as a unit, with no one part being more or less important than the rest. This flows directly out of his discussion of the *agape* meal in the previous chapter; Paul sees the same problem with spiritual gifts that he saw with their meal practices. The community was fragmenting itself needlessly because of divisions among itself. It is in the middle of this chapter that Paul, as a reminder, repeats that bit of baptismal liturgy: "For in the one Spirit we were all baptized into one body—Jews or Greeks, slaves or free—and we were all made to drink of one Spirit" (1 Cor. 12:13).

The third movement of this theme is the most powerful, and among the most poetic passages in the New Testament. Often known as "the love chapter," 1 Corinthians 13 is sometimes read at weddings, although it isn't really describing that kind of love. Instead, it's describing the kind of love that remedies the problems of 1 Corinthians 11 and 12—and the kind of love we should look to in our discussions of inclusion and justice. It's not an accident that Paul uses the word *agape* again and again in this chapter—eight times in thirteen verses. It's an intentional call-back to the *agape* meal in chapter 11, driving home the connection between patterns of inclusion and the love that binds the community together.

This is, as Paul puts it, "a still more excellent way" (1 Cor. 12:31b). It is a call to look and see who is excluded from our tables, and, on the principle of love, invite them to sit. It is a call to look at ourselves, and our selfish self-regard, and the chauvinistic roots of our exclusionary practices, and recognize that we are all part of the same body. These three movements on the same theme are Paul's most impassioned plea for just community and radical inclusion, and these passages easily overshadow the spare word or two that usually define Christian arguments about Paul's stance on LGBTQI persons. Plus, they also help us to interpret *malakoi* and *arsenokoitai*—by reminding us that whatever else Paul said, he instructed his communities to live according to the principle of love. Any interpretation of those words that doesn't flow out of love and lead back to love is wrong. Paul taught us that.

CHAPTER 4

Paul the Anti-Semite

Christian Violence

In the spring of my second year of divinity school, I took the required New Testament survey course. The lecture hall was filled with dozens of students, all working on a theological degree for one reason or another. Some were preparing to enter the nonprofit world or academia, but most of the students in the room were hoping to become ordained Christian clergy of some kind. Our professor was Amy-Jill Levine, a renowned scholar of the New Testament and a dynamic classroom teacher. Her lectures were always captivating, but on one particular day she had the class in thrall.

In hindsight, it must have been Holy Week, because Professor Levine's children were out of school, and they came to class with her that day. They sat in the back of the large theater-style classroom, quietly reading or doing their own homework as their mother lectured. As the end of class neared, though, Professor Levine began to climb the stairs to the back of the room where her son sat. She asked him to stand up. He was about ten years old at the time, still small next to his mother. She put her hand on his head, and she began to speak to us all. She knew, she told us, that many of us were training to become ministers, and that many of us were already serving in Christian congregations as interns or part-time staff. She wanted to remind us, she said, of the grave responsibility we held in those positions of authority, *especially* during the days leading up to Easter. Holy Week, when Christians remember and celebrate the events of the last week of Jesus' life, culminating in his crucifixion, has long been an occasion for Christian violence against Jews—violence in word and deed. From our own time and stretching back into the medieval period and to antiquity, Christians have read their own sacred scriptures' account of Jesus' suffering and death, and they have enacted violence against Jews.

Gospel stories about the Sanhedrin, Jesus' conflicts with Pharisees, and the crowd in Matthew that called out, "His blood be on us and on our children" (27:25b), have given Christians an excuse to engage in discrimination, verbal abuse, and pogroms. Standing there beside her son, Professor Levine asked us: "Never say anything from your pulpit that would cause harm to come to my Jewish boy."

It was a powerful moment, and I have never forgotten it. It was a reminder of the real-world stakes of biblical interpretation. The words in the Bible, when read and interpreted and acted upon, have consequences for people's lives. For centuries, one of the consequences of Christian biblical interpretation has been violence against Jews. Reading stories about Jesus' arguments with his fellow Jews, Christians have concluded that all Jews in their own day must be dishonest or theologically bankrupt. Reading stories about Jesus' crucifixion twenty centuries ago, Christians have decided that modern-day Jews must deserve the blame. Hearing sermons about the high priest Caiaphas and his role in Jesus' trial, Christians have walked out of church and rioted against their Jewish neighbors. There is a long and shameful history of Christian anti-Judaism and anti-Semitism, and the most horrific part of it came within living memory, in the Holocaust and its many horrors. Professor Levine's point on that spring afternoon was that biblical interpretation is never abstract, and that Christian violence has long been fueled by Christian scripture.

The biblical stories that have prompted and authorized Christian anti-Semitism have usually come from the gospels. But underneath those stories, less visible as sources of Christian anti-Semitism but at least as dangerous, have lurked other writings from the New Testament: the letters of Paul. Paul's writings—and stories about Paul from the Acts of the Apostles—are some of the most powerful sources of Christian bias against Jews. His letters have fueled Christian triumphalism and supersessionism for centuries, through misreadings of his comments about Jews and gentiles, Jewish law, and his own biography. And stories about Paul from Acts, especially the story of his experience on the road to Damascus, have helped create a persistent and pernicious malignancy within Christianity. Paul's life and writings have been used to create and perpetuate Christian anti-Semitic rhetoric, violence, and murder.

This history of Christian anti-Semitism rooted in Paul's life and teachings is tragically ironic because the Christian tradition —and Protestant Christianity in particular—has *completely* misunderstood Paul on this subject. Paul was not anti-Jewish, as so many Christians have understood and preached. He never rejected Jews or Judaism.

The persistent Christian belief that he *did* reject them is based on a centuries-old mistake. Whole theologies rest on a portrait of Paul that is deeply wrong, and those theologies have had real-world consequences for Jewish lives and communities. For over a generation now, biblical scholars have been overturning the bad exegesis that made these mistaken theologies possible. It's time for Christianity to repent of its anti-Semitic ways and claim Paul as an ally for dialogue and understanding with our Jewish sisters and brothers.

The Lutheran Perspective

Christians have been using scripture to justify violence against Jews for a long, long time, but especially since the Protestant Reformation we've been misreading and misusing Paul in a way that makes anti-Judaism and anti-Semitism even easier, and almost inevitable. Five hundred years after the Protestant Reformation, Protestant Christians can be justifiably proud of many things, but there is also much in that tradition for which we must atone. We need to rethink the way that we have portrayed Paul as anti-Jewish, and misinterpreted him as an opponent of Judaism. To understand why Paul has been so badly misunderstood, we begin with a little history.

The Protestant Reformation isn't a single event or act, but a series of events that unfolded over centuries. Its roots reach into the medieval church and attempts by some people to change that church. So the Reformation could be said to stretch into the early modern period, or even until today. But many historians point to one particular moment as what ignited the whole debate: Martin Luther's publication of the "95 Theses." Martin Luther is a towering figure in the Protestant Reformation, although he wasn't the first or the last reformer. He was a German Augustinian monk who gradually found himself more and more at odds with the Catholic Church, which was the dominant form of Christianity in that part of Europe. To make a long story short, Luther thought the church was corrupted by greed, plagued by inadequate and under-educated clergy, and theologically mistaken. He dedicated most of his adult life to attempting to fix, or "reform," the church, and a major part of that effort was his reorganization and reconstruction of Christian theology. It was this theological reform that led Martin Luther, in a roundabout way, to wield Paul as a weapon against Jews.[1]

Martin Luther had a problem: he was plagued by a sense of inadequacy before God. He famously lingered at confession, recounting every minor transgression to his confessor until he was finally sent

---

[1]Glenn S. Sunshine, *A Brief Introduction to the Reformation* (Louisville: Westminster John Knox Press, 2017), 13–24.

away. We will revisit this aspect of Luther's personality in the chapter 7 discussion on debt and guilt, because Luther's own tendency to dwell on sin steered him to understand Christianity in the same way, and that perspective persists to this day. For now, it's enough to know that Luther was convinced that sin was an overwhelming problem for humanity, and that it could only be solved by the faith of the believer and the grace found in the life, death, and resurrection of Jesus. The position that Luther developed has come to be known as the Lutheran Perspective, or Traditional Perspective. This Lutheran Perspective forms the foundation of much of Christian theology today, especially Protestant theology. But recall that it was founded on Luther's rejection of Catholicism.

Luther's big problem with the Catholic Church was that he felt it relied too much on "works" and not enough on grace. For Luther, "works" included a group of things that good Catholics did as demonstrations of piety and recompense for sin—from basic things such as prayer, pilgrimage, almsgiving, and penance, to more sensationalistic things such as purchasing *indulgences*: certificates that helped along one's own salvation or the salvation of someone else. Luther lumped all of these practices together (although he especially hated indulgences) in a criticism of what many people today call "works righteousness." So he went looking in scripture for arguments against works and in favor of faith. In the Judaism that is portrayed by the Jesus-following authors of the New Testament, Luther found a parallel to the Catholic Church he wanted to criticize, and he often compared Catholics to Jews in their supposed reliance on works, including legalistic adherence to standards of behavior.[2] Luther also found a kindred spirit in the pages of the New Testament: Paul. He read Paul as arguing for faith and against works, and therefore for Jesus and against the Jewish law. By making this comparison, Luther gained Paul as a powerful ally in his struggle against the Pope and the Catholic Church. But he also created a caricature of Judaism in the process, and he made Paul the natural enemy of Judaism and the standard-bearer of a new Lutheran Christianity, which opposed both Catholicism and Judaism.

The basic framework of how Luther used Paul in this way can be found in his preface to Romans in his monumental translation of the New Testament into German.[3] Romans is "truly the most important piece in the New Testament," Luther claims in his Introduction, and it

---

[2]James D. G. Dunn, "The Justice of God: A Renewed Perspective on Justification by Faith," *The Journal of Theological Studies* 43, no. 1 (April 1992): 1–22.

[3]Here and in all following quotations, I am using a translation by Bro. Andrew Thornton, OSB, which can be found online at https://www.ccel.org/l/luther/romans/pref_romans.html

is "purest gospel." Luther goes on to explain why this is true: because in Romans, Paul demonstrates that "works are a total loss and are completely useless," and that "faith alone makes someone just and fulfills the law." Justification before God happens through faith, Luther thinks Paul says, not through works. Luther goes on at length about Romans, of which—again—he is very fond. His enthusiasm for the book comes from his sense that he had found a true ally and fellow traveler in Paul. But, paired with that enthusiasm for Paul was a disdain for Jews and their supposed legalistic ways. In the same preface to Romans, commenting on chapter 2, Luther wrote, "Paul extends his rebuke to those who appear outwardly pious or who sin secretly," and quickly adds, "[S]uch were the Jews, and such are all hypocrites still, who live virtuous lives but without eagerness and love; in their heart they are enemies of God's law and like to judge other people."

Luther was playing on a very old Christian stereotype of Jews as hypocrites and illegitimate heirs of Abraham. Starting with the gospel writers, Christians often accused Jews of being hypocritical followers of the Jewish law—doers only, and not truly faithful. Christians leveled this charge for centuries, ignoring the very real problems with it as biblical interpretation, leading to outbreaks of ill will and even violence against Jews.[4] However, Luther elevated this anti-Jewish attitude until it became a precondition for salvation: if you want to be saved, Luther said, you cannot go about it anything like the Jews do. The very act of trying to do good works, he said, is harmful and wrong, when it is not accompanied by true faith (as he defined it). This was his reading of Paul, and it caused a great deal of harm to Jews in Luther's day and ever since. In the Protestant Reformation, Jews became the archetypal enemies of Christians, and Luther's readings of Paul served as the starting point.

Paul's "Conversion"

Yet this use of Paul's words in anti-Jewish and anti-Semitic rhetoric came not just from Paul's letters, but from another biblical source too: Paul's biographical details in the book of Acts. Three different times in Acts, the same basic story appears.[5] It begins with a man named Saul, who was harshly persecuting early followers of Jesus. Saul heard about some Jesus-followers in the city of Damascus, and so he set out to find them; but, on the way, something extraordinary happened. He

---

[4]For a great discussion of the problems with equating modern Jews with ancient ones, and the problems with reading gospel accounts of Pharisees uncritically, see chapter 7 of Pamela Eisenbaum, *Paul Was Not a Christian: The Original Message of a Misunderstood Apostle* (New York: HarperOne, 2009), 116–31.

[5]Acts 9:1–31; 22:1–21; and 26:9–18.

saw a light, was knocked to the ground, and heard a voice asking, "Saul, Saul, why do you persecute me?" The voice, which identified itself as Jesus, went on to tell Saul that from that point forward Saul was being charged with helping the Jesus-followers, not hindering them, and that he would be sent to the gentiles. After that, in the first telling of the story, Saul sought out the people he had been persecuting, and attempted to join them. They were understandably skeptical of him, and afraid, but eventually Saul joined forces with the early Christians and became Paul, the apostle to the gentiles.

This story is usually called "Paul's conversion," because it tells about how Paul stopped being one thing and started being another. For us, conversion describes a change of affiliation from one religion to another, and that's just what people mean when they talk about "Paul's conversion." They believe Saul stopped being Jewish and became Christian—and, to mark the occasion, he stopped being Saul and became Paul. It's a dramatic and tidy story—the pattern for conversion stories ever since—and it has had an incredibly powerful effect on our understanding of Paul and his mission.

Like many dramatic and "tidy" stories, though, there's more to this one than first meets the eye. Three things should give us pause when thinking about this "conversion" story. The first is that Paul's conversion could not have been as simple as we think, because in Paul's day the idea of a "conversion" wouldn't have made sense, and in any case there was no "Christianity" to which to "convert." The second is that after his experience on the road to Damascus, Paul showed no signs of having abandoned his Judaism in favor of a new religion; in fact, he continued to make strong statements about his Jewish identity and practice. The third is that we tend to think of Saul's name change to Paul as indicative of a big shift in identity, as with Abram's change to Abraham or Jacob's change to Israel. However, there is no indication in the story that Saul changed his name to Paul, and certainly not to signal a shift in identity. Instead, we can think of Paul's two names as a sign of Paul's struggle to fit in as part of the large and diverse Roman Empire, and to navigate the different parts of his world. I'll explain more about what I mean by each of these.

No Conversion and Nothing to Convert to

First, there is the problem of conversion. In our own time, many think of conversion in very straightforward terms. Conversion is the process by which you stop being one thing and start being another thing. Muslims can convert to Hinduism, Hindus can convert to Christianity, Christians can convert to Judaism, and so on. Many Christians think this way because they understand religion to be an all-or-nothing proposition; in our day, very few people hold more than one religious affiliation at a time. Many tend to think of religions as different rooms in the same house, or different paths up the same mountain. Those paths might cross on the way up, but that's about it—they never merge or join up. If you want to switch paths, you have to do so very intentionally, and you can't walk on two of them at the same time.

This is a relatively recent way of thinking about religion, though. In the ancient world, people didn't "convert" when they visited a new temple or participated in a new ritual to a new deity. They simply layered that practice or affiliation on top of the ones they already had.[6] In the ancient world, ordinary religious folk were constantly flabbergasted at Christians, who started insisting that *their* deity was the *only one* who should be worshiped, or the only one who existed at all! Paul, living at the very dawn of something we could call "Christianity," would not even have had any concept of "conversion." If you had asked him if he had converted, he would have been very confused. He would have responded that, as a Jew, he would never forsake the Jewish God. Even if, as did some Jews (and Christians), Paul had engaged in pagan practices *in addition to* his devotion to the Jewish God, it wouldn't have been a conversion. It would have been the normal, everyday layering and overlapping of religious practices that happened in the ancient world.

One more point on this first problem involving the concept of conversion: there was nothing to which to convert. Paul had his career in the 40s and 50s of the first century C.E., and he likely died in the early 60s. During this time, Christianity did not exist as a separate religion. At that point, Christianity hardly existed at all—it was made up of scattered small communities in large cities across the northern coast of the Mediterranean Sea, totaling maybe a few thousand people in all. There was no central organization, no agreed-upon rituals or sacred texts, and no common creed. Certainly there were the beginnings of all of these things, and Paul played a large role in that, but Christianity had not yet come onto the scene as anything we would call a "religion" today. Instead, anywhere you found them, Christians would have thought themselves to be—and would have been thought by outsiders to be—a sect of Judaism. You can see the traces of this sentiment all through the New Testament, and in other writings from the second century. The relationship between Jesus-followers and regular Jews was sometimes complicated and contentious—but because everyone assumed that these were different varieties of the same basic affiliation.

---

[6]A recent scholarly book on religion in the ancient world that is approachable to laypersons is Carlin A. Barton and Daniel Boyarin, *Imagine No Religion: How Modern Abstractions Hide Ancient Realities* (New York: Fortress, 2016).

Even for gentiles, who were Paul's main audience, the question was often how to integrate with an already-existing Jewish faith. Much of the book of Romans is about this question. As an example, the metaphor of the olive branch in Romans 11:17–24 presupposes a single tree onto which branches are being grafted, not a new separate tree. On the road to Damascus, Paul didn't convert, because there was nothing to which to convert.[7]

Paul's "Conversion" Away from Judaism

The second thing that should give us pause about this "conversion" story is that following his experience on the road to Damascus, Paul continued to live as a Jew, and engaged in all the practices one would expect of a Jewish person. In fact, all of his letters were written after this experience, and in those letters we find perhaps the most strident and proud declarations of Jewish identity of anyone from the ancient world. Paul was not just a regular Jewish person, he was an extremely proud Jewish person, and in his letters he sometimes made this point, forcefully. Romans 9:3–5, for example, is an extraordinary litany of positive attributes of Jewish identity, in which Paul affirms the special status of Israel before God. It begins somewhat confusingly, since verse 3 is somewhat unclear in the Greek: "For I could wish that I myself were accursed and cut off from Christ for the sake of my own people, my kindred according to the flesh." I like Robert Jewett's analysis of the verse. He says that Paul is likely mirroring texts such as Exodus 32:31–33, in which God and Moses have a conversation about the sin of Israel and Moses says that if God cannot forgive them, then God should blot Moses' own name "out of the book that you have written." So while at first glance this looks as if Paul is rejecting Israel, he is in fact defending Israel before God, which becomes clear in verses 4 and 5: "They are Israelites, and to them belong the adoption, the glory, the covenants, the giving of the law, the worship, and the promises; to them belong the patriarchs, and from them, according to the flesh, comes the Messiah, who is over all, God blessed forever." It's hard to imagine a more positive evaluation of Judaism than what Paul gives in this passage.

There are other good examples of Paul's passionate defense of his Jewish identity. One of these comes in 2 Corinthians 11:22, when he is talking about his opponents in Corinth: "Are they Hebrews? So am I... Are they descendants of Abraham? So am I." Here, Jewish identity is something akin to a credential on a resumé, a qualification for a task. Another related example is Galatians 1, which might be one of the

---

[7]For more on Paul's supposed "conversion," see Eisenbaum, *Paul Was Not a Christian*, 39–43.

angriest chapters in all of Paul's letters. This is partly because Paul seems to have heard a story that sounded something like the Acts accounts of his "conversion," and he emphatically sets the record straight. He tells the Galatians, contrary to Acts 9:10–30, "I did not confer with any human being, nor did I go up to Jerusalem to those who were already apostles before me" (1: 16b–17a). As part of his defense against this story, Paul writes in Galatians that he was a zealous Jew, and, "I advanced in Judaism beyond many among my people of the same age, for I was far more zealous for the traditions of my ancestors" (1:14). The passage begins with Paul describing his "earlier life in Judaism" (1: 13b), which some people have taken as a contrast to his present life in Christianity. But, *there was no Christianity*; Paul was contrasting his earlier life in Judaism to his later life in it. He was comparing the earlier part of his life, which was characterized by his persecution of Jesus-followers, to the period of his life he was in at present, when he wasn't persecuting them.

One final example drives the point home, and helps clarify some things about Paul's understanding of himself in relation to gentile Jesus-followers. In Philippians 3:2–9, Paul summarizes his message to his gentile audience, while at the same time underscoring his Jewish authority. The passage is worth reproducing in full:

> Beware of the dogs, beware of the evil workers, beware of those who mutilate the flesh! For it is we who are the circumcision, who worship in the Spirit of God and boast in Christ Jesus and have no confidence in the flesh—even though I, too, have reason for confidence in the flesh.

> If anyone else has reason to be confident in the flesh, I have more: circumcised on the eighth day, a member of the people of Israel, of the tribe of Benjamin, a Hebrew born of Hebrews; as to the law, a Pharisee; as to zeal, a persecutor of the church; as to righteousness under the law, blameless.

> Yet whatever gains I had, these I have come to regard as loss because of Christ. More than that, I regard everything as loss because of the surpassing value of knowing Christ Jesus my Lord. For his sake I have suffered the loss of all things, and I regard them as rubbish,[8] in order that I may gain Christ and be found in him, not having a righteousness of my own that comes from the law, but one that comes through faith in Jesus Christ, the righteousness from God based on faith.

---

[8]"Rubbish" translates the Greek word *skubala,* which has harsher and more scatological connotations than "rubbish." "Garbage," "crap," or even "shit" might be appropriate translations.

There is a lot going on in this passage. Paul seems to be arguing against "those who mutilate the flesh"—that is, those who insist that gentiles should be circumcised. This is because, for Paul, gentiles getting circumcised is a sign that they have missed the point. Gentiles don't need to get circumcised, because they don't need to become Jews. The whole point of Jesus is that Jesus' death and resurrection made salvation available to gentiles *as* gentiles; by trying to become Jewish, they try to "have...confidence in the flesh" rather than having confidence in Jesus. This is part of the resonance of the phrase "faith in Jesus Christ" near the end of the passage. Its meaning in Greek is far more complicated and controversial among scholars than most people know, and while it is usually translated here and in other places as "faith in Jesus Christ," it can just as easily be translated "faith *of* Jesus Christ" or "*faithfulness of* Jesus Christ" or even "*trustworthiness of* Jesus Christ."[9] In this passage, Paul is contrasting "confidence in the flesh" with the confidence gentiles can have in Jesus.

As part of this argument, Paul recites his own Jewish credentials in a way that mirrors what he did in 2 Corinthians 11. "Look," he is essentially saying, "I am as Jewish as the next guy. I'm impeccably Jewish. If I'm telling you not to get circumcised, but as a gentile to trust in Jesus' faithfulness; you can believe me." Again, Paul is listing his Jewishness as a credential or a source of authority. Paul is immensely proud of his Jewishness, and he sees it as the reason why people should listen to him. Far from abandoning his Judaism on the road to Damascus, Paul understands his Jewish identity as the bedrock of the thing he was called to do during that Damascus Road experience. His Jewishness isn't in the past, it's propelling him into the future. As Paul asks in another letter, "[H]as God rejected his people? By no means! I myself am an Israelite, a descendant of Abraham, a member of the tribe of Benjamin. God has not rejected his people whom he foreknew," and this is because, as he says later in the same chapter, "the gifts and the calling of God are irrevocable."[10]

Saul and Paul

The story of Paul's supposed "conversion" is usually told with a narrative flourish: he changed his name from Saul to Paul, as did some other people in the Hebrew Bible, to signify the change in identity. This

---

[9]We will revisit this problem in chapter 8. For a very scholarly and dense overview of this problem, see Richard B. Hays, *The Faith of Jesus Christ: The Narrative Substructure of Galatians 3:1—4:11*, 2d ed., The Biblical Resource Series (Grand Rapids, Mich.: Wm. B. Eerdmans, 2002).

[10]Romans 11:1–2a, 29. The "by no means" is an emphatic expression akin to "hell no" in English, which Paul uses especially when he has asked a rhetorical question to which he thinks the answer is obviously negative.

looks like a great proof for the "conversion" narrative, since it would draw a clear line between the past and the present—between the old Jewish Saul and the new Christian Paul. There's just one problem with this story: it didn't happen.

There's no biblical evidence for this name change at all, much less that the name change should be understood to mark off two separate religious affiliations: one pre-conversion and the other post-conversion. Neither Acts nor Paul's own letters ever talk about a name change, and there is absolutely no evidence that we are supposed to think about it as evidence of a religious conversion. If that were the point of the story, then we would expect the biblical texts to make a big deal about it, and for Paul to mention it in one of the credential-citing passages that we've looked at. Instead, there is nothing but silence about it.

Even the book of Acts is silent about the change. For the first half of Acts, only the name Saul was mentioned, but a shift happens at 13:9, in an unceremonious parenthetical passage featuring a magician named Elymas: "But Saul, also known as Paul,...looked intently at him" and proceeded to call him names and insult him. From that point forward in Acts, only the name Paul was used, with the exceptions of the passages in Acts 22 and 26, in which the Damascus Road story was told with its, "Saul, Saul, why do you persecute me?" quotation. Everywhere Saul went on the missionary journeys that fill the second half of Acts and that caused him to write his letters, he was known as Paul.

The best explanation for the two names of Paul is not a conversion story, but something else: Paul was doing something along the lines of "code-switching." Code-switching refers to the phenomenon in language in which a person uses one pattern of speech or dialect with one group of people, and another pattern or dialect with another group. People do this in order to fit in with their audience, and to signal to other people where they stand in relation to them. As an academic who is a native of southern Appalachia, I discovered early on that it was advantageous to code-switch in academic circles, because my southern accent, vocabulary, and patterns of speech often signaled (incorrectly, I hope) ignorance and lack of sophistication. On the other hand, my academic ways of talking give a similarly inaccurate impression to my friends and family when I talk to them. So, I switch "codes" to make myself as relatable and intelligible as possible to the people to whom I'm talking. Lots of people do this to overcome all sorts of biases, prejudices, and misconceptions among their audiences. People of color often feel they have to sound more "white" in job interviews, to overcome unjust misconceptions about their speech. Women are sometimes coached to "talk more like men"—using more assertive language, being less deferential—for the same reason, and politicians have mastered the art of code-switching at a moment's notice to appeal to a particular constituency.

We don't know whether Paul code-switched in his everyday language, because we don't have any examples of his writing to anyone other than churches and people he had encountered in his travels. It would be helpful if we had a letter he had sent to his grandmother, but we don't. All we have is his name switching, and that tells us that Paul was trying to make himself as acceptable and intelligible to the people he met and talked to as he could. "Saul," after all, was a very Jewish name. It was the name of the first king of Israel, King David's predecessor. Naming your child Saul would be something akin to naming your child George after George Washington—although Saul wasn't ultimately viewed as positively as Washington. But, outside of Jewish communities, the name Saul would have seemed strange and unclear. Many people wouldn't have known who King Saul was at all, and the ones who *did* know who he was would have tagged Paul immediately as a member of a strange colonized nation and sect on the edge of the Roman Empire. Right away they would have concluded that Paul was a nobody from nowhere. So, when he had been at home or near home, among family and fellow Jews, Saul had used his given name. However, once he ventured out into the Roman Empire (which he did in Acts 13, just a few verses after "Paul" appears for the first time in Acts), he went by Paul. "Paul," in contrast to "Saul," was a very "normal," very Roman name. Nobody would have batted an eyelid at someone named Paul. It's something like Barack Obama going by "Barry" early in life. It's a way to fit in, or at least to stand out less.

Paul tells us, in 1 Corinthians 9:20–22, that he does just this kind of code-switching to be more effective in his work: "To the Jews I became as a Jew... To those under the law I became as one under the law... To those outside the law I became as one outside the law... To the weak I became weak... I have become all things to all people..." It's not surprising that Saul would also change his name to make himself more relatable to his gentile audiences in Greece and Asia Minor. However, this is not the same thing as abandoning one identity for another, and it's certainly not evidence of a conversion away from Judaism and toward Christianity. It's just evidence that Paul took his work so seriously that he was willing to do whatever he needed to get it done.

Getting Paul Right: The New Perspective

The Lutheran Perspective, with its understanding of Paul as a person who converted away from legalistic works-based Judaism toward grace-based Christianity, has held sway for centuries. Especially among Protestant Christians, the understanding of Paul as the first, prototypical Christian has dominated, and with it has come the kind of rhetorical and physical violence that my professor warned us about in the story with which I started this chapter. Christian preaching and biblical interpretation *has* been a danger to Jews for a long time, and Professor Levine was right to worry for her son, and to worry about the kinds of damage that might come to him from the pulpit of a Protestant minister.

In recent years among Bible scholars, this Lutheran Perspective has been gradually losing support. In its place, something called the "New Perspective" has grown, so that in many biblical studies contexts, New Perspective adherents outnumber Lutheran Perspective supporters. Because it is so new, though, the New Perspective is still relatively unknown among Christian laypersons and even clergy, which is one of the reasons I am writing this book.[11] I think the New Perspective has the potential to help us rethink many different aspects of Christianity, and to make our modern interpretation of Christianity much more just and inclusive. But first the New Perspective needs to become more widely known, and it needs to dislodge the Lutheran Perspective as the default assumption of everyday Christians.

Because the New Perspective is so recent, not all scholars even agree on what it is, or what its goals ought to be. At the core, the New Perspective rests on the observation that Martin Luther and others similar to him misunderstood and misconstrued the Judaism of Paul's day. From there, though, several different understandings emerge of what conclusions to draw from that basic observation. I'll briefly talk about the central New Perspective observation about the Judaism of Paul's day, and then sketch one of the main options for what the New Perspective might look like or accomplish: the Radical New Perspective. Then, I'll provide my own take on how the Radical New Perspective can help us rethink Paul's Jewishness and Christianity's relationship to Judaism in a way that makes our tradition less anti-Semitic and anti-Jewish.

Rethinking Ancient Judaism with the New Perspective

Martin Luther wanted to criticize the Catholic Church for being too works-focused, so he made a comparison to an ancient Judaism that was works-focused, and made Paul (and Jesus) its enemy. This move served Luther very well as a rhetorical sword to swing at his Catholic

---

[11]The work of Paula Fredriksen, Pamela Eisenbaum, E.P. Sanders, Krister Stendahl, James D.G.Dunn, Mark Nanos, Marcus Zetterholm, and affiliated scholars provide a good starting point for exploring this burgeoning field of biblical studies.

opponents. But, in the process, Luther made anti-Judaism and anti-Semitism cornerstones of his theology, worsening a tendency that had already long been evident in Christianity. Beyond that, though, Luther also perpetuated and popularized stereotypes about ancient Judaism that were misleading or just plain wrong. Correcting those mistakes is the principle shared by all forms of the New Perspective, and is the first step toward less-harmful Christian theologies.

One of the earliest major books to take on these misunderstandings and falsehoods was *Paul and Palestinian Judaism* by E.P. Sanders, published in 1977.[12] In it, Sanders pointed out how thoroughly the layers of Christian theology and polemic had obscured our understanding of the Judaism of Paul's day. The impression of Judaism one got from Luther and subsequent Christian theology was of a legalistic, works-based religion, but when you looked at the actual Jewish sources from that time, a very different picture emerged. The Judaism described by Luther and his heirs was hardly recognizable; instead, you found a vibrant, covenantal relationship between God and Israel, structured by law, yes, but also by grace. This ought not to surprise us! After all, Jesus and Paul were both Jews of this period. The ideas of Jesus and Paul were not huge departures from the ideas of other Jews of the same period. The New Perspective rests on this foundation.

I consider myself to be a part of a subsection of scholars within the New Perspective that is sometimes called the Radical New Perspective, and goes farther in protecting Paul's Jewish identity and separating out God's plans for Jews and gentiles. According to this Radical New Perspective on Paul, one huge problem drove Paul: gentiles. In this way of thinking, Paul thought that he was living in or on the cusp of an eschatological age—a critical time when God was preparing to intervene in history to end the world or change it in some radical way. The death and resurrection of Jesus was a sign that this new age was upon them. Israel, in this apocalyptic scenario, had nothing to worry about, because they were in a covenantal relationship with God. Despite the sometimes rocky nature of that relationship, grace characterized God's love for Israel, and Paul had no concerns about himself and his fellow Jews. However, gentiles were adrift, exposed in the world without the protection afforded to Israel. The death and resurrection of Jesus had opened a door, Paul thought, but someone had to tell the gentiles to walk through it. Paul believed that someone was him.

In this Radical New Perspective, Paul's problem with the Jewish law wasn't that it was inadequate, as the Lutheran Perspective suggests. The

---

[12]E. P. Sanders, *Paul and Palestinian Judaism: A Comparison of Patterns of Religion* (Philadelphia: Fortress, 1977).

Jewish law and the Jewish covenant were plenty adequate—for *Jews*. But, the law didn't protect gentiles, who were the ones Paul felt called to reach. Therefore, when Paul criticized the law in his writings, he did so because he felt that it left gentiles "out in the cold." The solution to this problem of the law's exclusivity was Jesus, and Paul hit upon a phrase—"justification by faith"—to describe how the Jewish God was being made available to gentiles through Jesus.[13] Paul's audience in his letters, in this way of seeing things, was the gentile population, and that's why he's sometimes seen criticizing the law. If we had letters Paul wrote to fellow Jews, he might have said something different; however, for gentiles Paul needed to make it clear that justification by faith, and not adherence to the law, was the path to salvation.

The Radical New Perspective is often criticized because of how it implies that there are two ways of salvation—one for Jews, and one for gentiles. Many interpreters, especially people formed and informed by Christian categories and theologies, simply cannot imagine that Paul would have believed in two ways of salvation. Jesus, after all, is famously quoted in the Gospel of John as saying, "I am the way, and the truth, and the life" (14:6). Christians have usually taken the definite article "the" to imply that Jesus is the *only* way of salvation, and that any other way of salvation must be illegitimate. When I was a teenager, I worked at an evangelical summer camp, and I can remember getting into arguments about just this topic. My more normative evangelical friends would argue that Jews were not "saved," and were in danger of going to hell unless they became believers in Jesus. Meanwhile, I pointed to the covenants God made with Israel in the Bible, and stood on the principle that God does not break covenants. Humans might violate covenants, I reasoned, but if God was in the business of breaking covenants, we were all in a lot of trouble. I was therefore articulating a two-ways system of salvation, which drove my friends crazy. But, I saw no reason why God couldn't keep two promises at once.

That might be why it doesn't bother me so much now that the Radical New Perspective suggests two ways of salvation. The Bible itself suggests that there are at least two ways (and maybe more, depending on how you count), and I think Paul likely would have had a robust understanding of God's freedom to save in whatever way God thought best, and that God was not limited by any cosmic non-compete agreement. One of my favorite scholars, Krister Stendahl, calls this "God's traffic plan," in which Israel was brought in first, and gentiles

---

[13]Remember, though, that "faith" in Paul's writings could just as easily refer to Jesus' own faithfulness or trustworthiness, and not necessarily the believer's faith *in* Jesus.

second.[14] Later on in the same book, Stendahl takes on the notion that salvation could occur through the process of everyone coming into line with each other—through everyone becoming the same. That, he says, "is the climax of Christian condescension."[15] I agree, which is why I see so many possibilities in the Radical New Perspective, both for reimagining old models of salvation (which will be the topic of chapter 7) and for improving Jewish-Christian relations. Or, to put it differently, I see the Radical New Perspective as a much-needed correction to centuries of anti-Semitic and anti-Jewish theologies. Once we start reading Paul with the Radical New Perspective, he stops being an enemy of his own people, and he begins to offer us resources for rethinking Christian theology in a more expansive and inclusive way.

Paul the Proud Israelite and Christian Apostle

One of the basic difficulties with reading Paul is that he sometimes writes confusing or even contradictory things. How can Paul write so glowingly about his own Jewish identity, citing it like a qualification of which he's very proud, and at the same time write so harshly about the Jewish law? One solution is to conclude that Paul can't be trusted; he's either too inconsistent or too incompetent in his knowledge of the Jewish law to be a reliable narrator about it.[16] A much older way of dealing with this difficulty comes from the Lutheran Perspective, which understands Paul's boasting about his Jewishness to belong to his now-forsaken past, and his reservations about the Jewish law to belong to his present and future as a Christian. Both of these solutions are unsatisfying, though, because the one makes Paul into the kind of fool that the evidence doesn't support, and the other divides Paul into two people, one on either side of the Damascus Road experience. Both solutions make him out to be a very bad and marginal member of the nation of Israel, a charge to which Paul would have objected strongly— and did repeatedly in his letters.

The Radical New Perspective solves this problem, and at the same time it offers a new vision of Paul that will be welcome to progressive Christians. No longer is Paul the anti-Semite. No longer is he the zealous Jew who converted away from his faith and spent the rest of his life lobbing grenades at the Jewish law. Instead, in the Radical New Perspective, Paul is a proud Israelite, confident and even boastful about his Jewishness. And, at the same time, he is Christianity's most energetic and successful messenger of Jesus Christ, spreading the good

---

[14]Krister Stendahl, *Final Account: Paul's Letter to the Romans* (Minneapolis: Fortress, 1995), 7.

[15]Ibid., 39.

[16]Eisenbaum, *Paul Was Not a Christian*, 214.

news from Jerusalem to at least as far west as Rome. Paul didn't see any conflict between these two identities, and neither should we. He was a Jewish man with a deep and deeply felt concern for gentiles, who he thought were at risk of perishing apart from God. He was also an enthusiastic follower of Jesus, undergoing much suffering and entering into much danger on behalf of the cause. Paul was undoubtedly a complicated man, but in this regard he was simple: he was a zealous Jew who devoted his life to a Jewish messiah who had come to save gentiles.

CHAPTER 5

Paul the Prude

"True Love Waits" Sunday

When I was a teenager, I arrived at church one Sunday morning with my family, not suspecting the ambush that awaited me. I loved my little church. I had started attending a few years earlier at the invitation of a friend, whose father was the pastor, and soon my whole family had joined and we attended almost every Sunday. I was a junior deacon, active in the youth group, and part of a healthy Sunday school class. I even enjoyed worship; the pastor was an excellent preacher, and his sermons often gave me lots to think about, and I grew to love the traditional hymns and songs the small choir sang. However, on that one particular Sunday, something different happened at church. It was "True Love Waits" Sunday.

Many people about my age and from similar church backgrounds will know all about "True Love Waits." It was (and still is) a fixture of Christian purity culture, and in the 1990s when I was a teenager, True Love Waits was just beginning to become popular. I had heard about True Love Waits, but I had never given it much thought before. About halfway through worship that Sunday, though, I learned a lot more about it. Unbeknownst to me, that particular Sunday the church had planned a kind of ritual. I was handed a pledge card, as were the other half-dozen or so teenagers in the congregation that morning. I was told that there would be a moment during the service when I would be invited to come forward, with my parents, and sign the card in front of the congregation. I don't have the pledge card anymore, but I looked up some old ones online, and I'm fairly certain that the language on mine matched this one:

> Believing that true love waits, I make a commitment to God, myself, my family, my friends, my future mate and my future

children, to a lifetime of purity including sexual abstinence from this day until I enter a biblical marriage relationship.[1]

There was a place for me to sign the card, which I did. My parents and I were then invited to come up the center aisle of the church, to the front of the sanctuary, and to make a commitment to my sexual purity until marriage. I remember it being very awkward, and I remember exchanging knowing looks with my fellow teenagers, there at the front of the church. No matter how pious you are, no teenager wants to stand up in front of their congregation with their parents while their sexual purity is discussed. There were words said—I don't remember what, exactly—and perhaps a prayer spoken, and then my parents and I returned to our seats. We never spoke about it again.

I was definitely on board with the goals of True Love Waits; by then I was immersed in evangelical subculture, and abstinence before marriage was a big part of that. I had already heard the message that sex was something best preserved for marriage. I was also in no danger of compromising my sexual purity. I was an awkward and gangly teenager who didn't date and had little interest in trying to. Most likely, my life without the True Love Waits pledge would have looked very much like my life with it; it would be another half a decade before there was any serious threat to my chastity. Even though that was true, and even though I agreed with the principles behind it, I still felt ambushed and betrayed by True Love Waits, by my pastor, and by my church. It felt like something very personal and private had been made the object of public scrutiny and moralizing.

Now, decades later, I can appreciate how much more painful and invasive it must have felt to other people—to girls who were shamed for how they looked or how they acted, to people engaging in healthy and age-appropriate romantic activities who were suddenly viewed with suspicion, and of course to people who didn't conform to Christianity's constructions of gender or sexuality. I was a straight boy, one of the most normative kinds of people in my small town, and *even I* felt singled out and picked on. I can't imagine how others felt. Well, in some cases I can, because my friends today have sometimes told me how hurtful their own encounters with Christian purity culture were. That line on the pledge card, "from this day forward," took on threatening tones for anyone who was known or suspected to have engaged in sexual activity already; for them, the pledge was more than just an agreement to put off sex until marriage, it was a condemnation of their present morality. I know people whose teenage years were spent trying to manage the

---

[1]Rosie Franklin, "True Love Doesn't Wait," *Disrupting Dinner Parties: Feminism for Everyone* (blog), March 22, 2013, https://disruptingdinnerparties.com/2013/03/22/truelovedoesntwait/.

harmful interplay of their bodies, their social and family lives, and the claims of Christian purity culture.

Paul, unfortunately, was a big part of all of this, and he still is. Anyone who has passed through the True Love Waits program, or anyone who has encountered Christian purity culture in other forms, has probably had Paul's writings thrown at them. Programs such as True Love Waits tend to draw heavily on the writings of Paul, and writings attributed to him. I can remember a few verses from other books of the Bible being quoted to me (Song of Songs 8:4 seems to have been a favorite), but most of the major proof texts for chastity culture came from Paul, and especially from Romans and 1 Corinthians. The words will be familiar to many of you: "[Y]our body is a temple of the Holy Spirit"; "[I]t is well for a man not to touch a woman"; "Put to death, therefore, whatever in you is earthly: fornication, impurity, passion, evil desire, and greed"; "[M]ake no provision for the flesh, to gratify its desires"; and "[P]resent your bodies as a living sacrifice, holy and acceptable to God."[2] These, and others similar to them, have formed the backbone of abstinence and purity efforts, turning Paul into a prude and a scold in the minds of many people. One of the first things many people say to me when I tell them I study Paul is that he must have had some kind of repressed sexual dysfunction because he talked about sex so frequently. Even though Paul doesn't talk about sex all the time in his writings, people get the impression that he does, because of the outsized emphasis placed on his writings by programs such as True Love Waits. Having been through my own experience with True Love Waits and having heard lots of Paul quoted to me scoldingly over the years, I can understand why.

Paul and Purity

Although it's not true that he wrote about sex constantly, as many people think, the writings of Paul are a gold mine for anyone looking for biblical passages on the subject. We could start with the vice lists we looked at back in chapter 3, which mention "fornication" prominently as one of the things to shun. However, there are a lot of other passages too. Large portions of 1 Corinthians deal with sexuality; in a series of sections in chapters 5, 6, and 7, Paul takes on issues from prostitution to marital relations to the strange situation between a man and his father's wife in 5:1. Chapter 7 in particular has proven tricky for popular interpreters and biblical scholars alike; in 7:1–6, Paul seems to be advocating for a mutuality of sex in married relationships, but in the next breath (7:7–9) he seems to suggest that it's better not to marry

---

[2] 1 Corinthians 6:19; 1 Corinthians 7:1; Colossians 3:5; Romans 13:14; Romans 12:1.

at all. Academics argue over whether the position in 7:1, "It is well for a man not to touch a woman," is Paul's position or him quoting the Corinthian position. Even though the latter is probably true, and Paul is actually arguing *against* the idea that men should avoid touching women, many Christians have taken this passage to mean that sexual abstinence is the best approach.

In Romans 6:12 and following, Paul ruminates on the relationship between sin and bodies, and the need for bodily control. Later in Romans, in chapter 13, Paul wraps up his argument about governing authorities by instructing his readers to "make no provision for the flesh, to gratify its desires," which lends itself nicely to chastity arguments. In both Romans 14:13 and 1 Corinthians 8:9, Paul warns against placing a stumbling block in front of people. This is an allusion to Leviticus 19:14, which is about kindness toward people with disabilities, but many purity advocates use it to shame women and girls into dressing and acting modestly so that they don't provoke the sexual desires of men and boys. (Men and boys, in this view, seem to be incapable of avoiding this particular stumbling block, and are passive victims of female sexuality.)

Galatians 5:13 is another verse often taken out of its context to apply to sexual morality: "For you were called to freedom, brothers and sisters; only do not use your freedom as an opportunity for self-indulgence, but through love become slaves to one another." In the context of Galatians, this fits in with a larger argument that Paul is making about the Galatians' relationship with God, but many have seen it as a warning about what you *should* do with your body, as opposed to what you *could* do. A few verses later, in 5:16, Paul tells the Galatians to "[l]ive by the Spirit...and do not gratify the desires of the flesh." This leads nicely into the vice list in 5:19–21, in which fornication and impurity figure prominently. In 1 Thessalonians 4:3–8, Paul admonishes his readers to abstain from fornication, to control their bodies, and to avoid lustful passions similar to those that gentiles indulge.

Not to be outdone, even the pseudo-Pauline material includes passages similar to these. In a small vice list in Colossians 3:5, the author instructs the reader to "[p]ut to death, therefore, whatever in you is earthly," and the first three things on the list are "fornication, impurity, [and] passion." Also, 2 Timothy 2:22 is especially useful for youth pastors and others who are attempting to control teenage sexuality: "Shun youthful passions and pursue righteousness," it reads, and it's easy to see how that could be used to apply to sex, especially the "youthful" kind that makes adults panicky.

What accounts for the heavy use of Paul's writings in arguments about sexual purity? Why is Paul such a rich source of passages about bodies and relationships, and why do so many of his words get used to enforce standards of purity similar to those found in True Love Waits? I think there are two main reasons. The first is that there aren't very many other parts of the Bible that are useful sources on the subject of sexuality, and the second is that Paul's focus on gentile immorality is easily plucked from its historical context and applied uncritically to modern sexuality.

Regarding the first, the fact that there are few other parts of the Bible that are useful as texts about sexuality is under-appreciated by most readers of the Bible. The Bible is often silent about human sexuality, and when it does give advice or commands about sex, those commands are sometimes at odds with what modern Christians think of as normative sexuality. Christians tend to think of the Bible as a sourcebook or handbook for any kind of question or problem, but that is not at all what the Bible is or wants to be. It does not systematically approach the question of human sexuality. Jesus rarely mentions sex, outside of the occasional reference to fornication, as in Mark 7:21 or Matthew 15:19. The John 8 story of the woman caught in adultery is rightly famous, but that story is much more about grace and humility than it is about restrictions on sex. It's not really a story about adultery at all, but one about the *response* to adultery and the human impulse to judge others' actions more harshly than our own.

The Hebrew Bible (or Old Testament) is not much help either. There are plenty of models of relationships in the Hebrew Bible, but many of those are models of polygamous marriages, marriages begun by rape or conquest, arranged marriages, marriages that look more like business deals, or the kind of sexual trickery found in the stories of Rahab, Tamar, and Ruth. The story of David and Bathsheba has given rise to one of the most overdone songs of our time, Leonard Cohen's *Hallelujah*, but in the biblical text that's a story of deceit, murder, and abuse of power that doesn't play very well in the #metoo era. The Song of Songs (or Song of Solomon) is the most love-and-sex-focused book of the Hebrew Bible, and for that reason it has always faced questions about whether it belongs in the canon at all, or whether it's really an allegory for something much holier, such as God and the world or Christ and the church, rather than a man and a woman who are infatuated with each other and desiring each other. I can remember sitting through a few months' worth of Monday night meetings of the Fellowship of Christian Athletes, viewing a video series on sex that was based on the Song of Songs. The message that was remarkably wrung from Song of Songs? Don't have sex.

But that course on the Song of Songs was the exception. The reason you don't see True Love Waits quoting many of these texts is that they don't fit very well in the purity paradigm. The story of Jacob and Rachel might seem to be a good model to teach young people about the merits of "traditional marriage"— until one remembers that Jacob was also in simultaneous relationships with Rachel's sister Leah, a woman named Bilhah, and a fourth woman named Zilpah, that he essentially purchased the first two women from their father in exchange for years of labor, or that the last two women likely had little say about their sexual relationship with Jacob.

One of the dirty secrets of the idea of "biblical marriage," as referenced in the True Love Waits pledge card I signed as a teenager, is that "biblical marriage" often looked nothing like the "purity" imagined by modern Christians. True Love Waits doesn't usually cite Deuteronomy 22:23–24, even though those verses describe punishing both participants in a pre-marital sex act, and 22:28–29 isn't cited either, even though that passage references lifelong marriage without divorce. These stories aren't cited because the first one ends in the death penalty for both participants, and the second one is explicitly about rape. "Biblical marriage" is not a category with much integrity; the actual marriages in the Bible don't look very much like the model that was put in front of me as a teenager, or the one that's given to many young people today.

The Hebrew Bible isn't very helpful, and the gospels aren't either, so most of what's left comes from Paul. This leads me to the second reason in regards to why Paul's writings are so useful for arguments about sexual purity: because one of the major focal points of his writing was the problem of gentile immortality. *Remember:* Paul was writing to gentiles, and gentiles were his career's major concern. He wasn't writing to his fellow Jews, who he seems to have felt had a pretty good handle on sexual mores and prohibitions (even if they didn't always follow them). Paul was writing to people that he (and his fellow Jews) already thought were inclined to be sexually unrestrained. The Jewish stereotype about gentiles was that they were likely to engage in all sorts of sexual behaviors that the Jewish law prohibited, and Paul bought into that stereotype completely. His experiences with communities such as the one in Corinth must have confirmed his prejudices. Remember that 1 Corinthians contains a long section with passage after passage of Paul addressing sexual improprieties. You can almost hear the frustration and disbelief in his voice coming through his writing as he names, one by one, the activities he has heard about in the church at Corinth. The Corinthians were confirming everything Paul had always heard and suspected about the gentiles.

This is really what's going on in most of these texts from Paul: he is introducing, reiterating, and enforcing norms from the Jewish law for his gentile audience. Paul *didn't* think that gentiles needed to follow the Jewish law as a way to become Israelites and enter a relationship with the Jewish God. Paul was actually very offended by that idea. One of the insights of the New Perspective on Paul, and particularly the Radical New Perspective, is that Paul very much wanted gentiles to "stay in their lane." He wanted them to remain gentiles, because that was the status under which they were being saved, through the faithfulness of Jesus. Following the law in order to gain salvation was a bad idea and an affront to the saving work of Jesus. But, Paul *did* think that it was a good idea for gentiles to follow *some* aspects of the Jewish law. He didn't want them to do this just to gain salvation, but for another reason as well: to protect the church, as the body of Christ, from pollution.

The argument that Paul wanted to protect the body of Christ from pollution can be found in a wonderful book by Dale Martin called *The Corinthian Body*.[3] It's a creative and engaging book that uses ancient ideas about bodies to help understand 1 Corinthians, and I encourage you to read it. As Martin says, Paul thought of bodies in a way that was somewhat different from that of some of the people in the church in Corinth, and that difference helps us understand why something such as the situation described in 1 Corinthians 6:15 would bother Paul so much. It's not simply the violation of the norms of Jewish law that bothered Paul when a member of the church visited a prostitute, although that was certainly a part of it. It was that the church member was introducing a permeability to the church's body, by which something from outside could enter in. For Paul, basic morality ought to be enough to prevent someone from visiting a prostitute, but, in case it wasn't, he also wanted to emphasize the person's obligation to the community. Paul thought that the community of believers in Jesus functioned as a body, and he used that metaphor in both 1 Corinthians and Romans. If it was true that the church was the body of Christ, he reasoned, then a person's sexual behavior wasn't just about themselves, but about the whole community, and about Jesus himself. Perhaps a similar idea was at play when my childhood church planned their True Love Waits pledge card signing, and that was why it was done in the presence of the whole community, with my parents playing a prominent role. The language of contagion and sanctity is certainly part of the rhetoric of Christian purity movements.

Beyond the basic morality of Jewish law, though, and beyond this concern about the susceptibility of the body of Christ to invasion and pollution, there was something else going on with Paul's discussions of

---

[3]Dale B. Martin, *The Corinthian Body* (New Haven, Conn.: Yale University Press, 1995), 163–97.

sexuality that we have to understand. This was a basic understanding that Paul had of the world that most of us don't share, and it strongly influenced his writing about sexuality. Without this understanding of the world (which turned out to be incorrect) Paul might never have written some of the most troublesome parts of his letters, including 1 Corinthians 7, in which he talks about marriage, singleness, and celibacy. There was a particular reason for Paul's emphasis on celibacy: he thought the world was about to end.

It's the End of the World as We Know It (And Paul Feels Celibate)

One of the key principles of the Radical New Perspective is that you always have to read Paul with his eschatology in mind. Paul was convinced that Jesus' life, death, and resurrection were decisive events in history, inaugurating the beginning of a new era, and signaling the imminent intervention of God into the world and the second coming of Jesus. Paul thought that these events would take place in his own lifetime; you can see this in his earliest letter, 1 Thessalonians. Chapter 4 of that letter reveals that when he was in Thessaloniki, Paul had been preaching an extremely imminent eschaton. The Thessalonians were so convinced of the immediacy of these events that when some among them died before Jesus had returned, they panicked. Had the promises of God failed? Had Jesus been delayed? Had Paul been wrong? They had apparently asked Paul about this in a letter or by messenger, because he wrote back to them with an answer, beginning in 4:13: "But we do not want you to be uninformed, brothers and sisters, about those who have died, so that you may not grieve as others do who have no hope." Paul goes on to explain that while some might have indeed died, they will still have their place. In fact, he says, "the dead in Christ will rise first," and "[t]hen we who are alive, who are left, will be caught up in the clouds together with them to meet the Lord in the air" (vv. 16–17a). (This, by the way, is the sole scriptural justification for the so-called "rapture," which, contrary to popular belief, does not appear in the book of Revelation.)

So, Paul was expecting the eschaton soon, in his own lifetime, and that expectation left a deep impression on his ethics. Think about every apocalyptic movie you have ever seen. When the disaster is coming—an invasion of space aliens, a zombie horde, an asteroid—people behave differently. Things that would matter in a world that would keep on turning, suddenly matter a lot less. People quit their jobs, gamble away their money, engage in risky behaviors, and fall into deep depressions or high hopes (depending on their perspectives), because the shortened timeline of their lives has put things into a new light. The same was true for Paul. He thought that Jesus' return would happen any minute, which is why he had such urgency about his missionary journeys across the Mediterranean world, and such impatience for people and communities who didn't share his sense of motivation. He wanted to bring the gentiles into the fold before the end came and they were left out in the cold. But, beyond influencing his missionary work, Paul's shortened timeline had another effect: it made his ethics tragically short-sighted.

We will see one example of this in chapter 6 of this book, because in that chapter we will see that Paul told enslaved people to remain enslaved. Because he thought time was so short, he said that it would do no good to try to change their lot in life; Jesus was returning soon anyway, so best to focus on that and all that came with it, rather than emancipation or escape. But there was one very pronounced effect of Paul's short eschatology: he didn't think it was worthwhile at all to concede any time to durable interpersonal relationships such as marriages, because they would become irrelevant the moment Jesus returned. For Paul, marriage was the kind of thing that was best avoided, given the (perceived) situation, because it could only distract from the work of bringing in the gentiles and the focus on personal devotion to Jesus. If there was time for only one thing, Paul knew what that one thing should be, and it wasn't planning a wedding.

I'd mentioned that the beginning of 1 Corinthians 7 is confusing, because while it looks as if Paul is making a personal statement when he says, "It is well for a man not to touch a woman," he is probably actually restating a question that had been asked of him by the Corinthians. They wanted to know: What should we do about sex? Humans are, after all, physical beings, and the Corinthians might have found themselves stuck between their best intentions to abide by Paul's instructions on the one side, and their human nature on the other side. They wrote to Paul to ask exactly what he meant by all the "don't touch women" business, because the issue had apparently become urgent for some of them. Celibacy was a fine ideal for a few weeks or months—but it had been years by the time they wrote to Paul to ask about his teaching, and some of them were starting to question the wisdom of the approach. It's worth noting that we don't actually know Paul's precise position on the matter. The quote, "It is well for a man not to touch a woman," in 7:1 might have been what Paul had said about the matter during his time in Corinth, but it might also have been a phrase of some members of the Corinthian community who took Paul's general guidance too seriously or strictly.

In either case, Paul's response is a moderating one, even though in some places it looks strict to us today. He begins by making a concession to human nature: marriage is probably inevitable, because without it there would be too much sexual immorality. And, within marriage, Paul says, husbands and wives should give "conjugal rights" to each other. (Paul did not contemplate marriages that weren't between a man and a woman.) On the one hand, this is a strange and somewhat uncomfortable thing for Paul to say. He's arguing for marriage, but only as a way to contain runaway sexuality, and he's saying that people within marriages automatically owe each other sex, which definitely does not fit with most progressive Christians' values today.

However, on the other hand, you can see how Paul is a little bit stuck here. He believes that the world is going to end, and very soon, and that people should have the self-control to focus on their religious transformation, and not waste time on relationships and sex. That is the choice he has made; he has turned away from any desire he might have had, and has focused on the mission he has been given by God. But, on the other hand, he recognizes human nature for what it is, and concedes that, for most people, sex is probably going to happen. Given human nature, Paul thinks that marriage is better than no marriage. "I wish that all were as I myself am," Paul writes in 7:7. He wishes, in other words, that everyone was celibate. "But each has a particular gift from God, one having one kind and another a different kind," he adds, suggesting that, for some people, abstinence is simply not their gift.

This passage sums up the difficulty of Paul for me. He almost always has good intentions, and he also has a pastoral sensibility about him, so that he understands that not everybody can be like him. But, he also has a strong sense of self-regard, and a real impatience for people who lack the laser focus on mission that he seems to have. He recognizes that not everyone shares his dispositions, yet he can't help but impose some of his dispositions on others. He knew that his people in Corinth struggled to keep the same kinds of practices that he kept, yet he still asked them to be as much like him as they could. When we read this exchange nineteen centuries later, we struggle to locate ourselves in it.

This leads to the most important caveat of all for anyone trying to read Paul as a source of ethics: *Paul was not trying to write ethics for all people in every time and place.* When he wrote 1 Corinthians 7, Paul meant it for the Corinthians in the middle of the first century. He had in mind their particular struggles and successes. When he wrote to them about husbands and wives, he probably had particular couples in mind. When, later in the chapter, he talked about virgins, he probably knew the names of the people about whom he was writing. "Oh, yes,...

Larry...yes, it's probably best if Larry goes ahead and gets married." None of this was abstract for Paul. This was very particular advice, given to people he knew in very known circumstances. The fact that he was adjusting his advice on the fly and responding to changing circumstances—the whole reason for 1 Corinthians 7 to be written at all—tells us that he was not dogmatic and unchanging, but instead willing to shift and adjust his advice based on changing events. He knew that some of his people in Corinth would struggle with sexual immorality, and so he advocated marriage for those people. He knew others were more like him, capable of celibacy, and he gave them a space to live too. What he didn't know at all was that his letter to them would become scripture, and that it would be read by people like us thousands of years later. He didn't anticipate anything about our world, other than basic human nature, which hasn't changed very much since his time.

Paul didn't anticipate people like us, because he didn't think the world would exist long enough. This is clear later in chapter 7 when, in verse 20, he tells people to "remain in the condition in which you were called," and not try to change the status of their circumcision. In the next verse, he tells slaves to remain as slaves, and not try to change their station. The same is true for relationships in 26–31: "I think that, in view of the impending crisis, it is well for you to remain as you are," and a few lines later, explains "the appointed time has grown short." Paul was not constructing ethics for the long haul, to be equally applicable in the first century, and the tenth century, and the age of Tinder. He was a Jewish missionary to gentiles—people he thought had little capacity for self-control. He thought the world was ending soon, or at least radically changing, and that it made very little sense to attempt to change one's station in life, including one's relationship status. He didn't see the value in marriage as a long-term institution. For Paul, marriage was essentially a safety net for humans' uncontrollable urges: if his gentile Corinthian Jesus-followers couldn't control their libidos, then they should at least be married, so they could indulge their urges there.

Are We Reading Paul Fairly?

Modern Christian purity movements such as True Love Waits, along with the broader world of Christian teaching about sexuality, consider one interpretation of Paul among many. In my opinion, they get some things right about Paul, and other things wrong. The notion of Paul as a prude is not *completely* wrong. Paul understood human sexuality as a destructive force that had to be contained, and he thought that certain people, such as gentiles, were less capable of controlling that sexuality. Christian purity culture also thinks that human sexuality is a destructive force that needs to be controlled by strict limits on sexual behaviors, and that certain kinds of people, such as teenagers, are more susceptible to it. Both Paul and modern purity culture see marriage as an ideal. Both rely on pre-existing stereotypes, which are often unexamined, to construct ideals of sexual behavior. Both have ramifications for gender equity that make us squeamish, and both have led to abuse in unfortunate and unholy ways.

While there are parallels, though, there are also significant differences. Those differences have a lot to do with the differences between Paul and us, and they help to nuance that view of Paul as a prude. Paul lived in antiquity and had a limited understanding of biology and psychology, and he had narrow interests in mind when he wrote letters such as 1 Corinthians. Those of us who live in the modern world have deeper knowledge and broader possibilities. Science has revealed far more about human sexuality than anyone in Paul's day ever imagined, and we are much more aware of the variety of expressions of human sexuality than Paul ever was. In one sense, we even have a much fuller perspective on Paul's letters than he did; while he thought he was writing to Corinthians or Romans or Thessalonians at the very end of time, we know that he was in fact writing to the whole world, and that his writings would continue to be read for thousands of years. When we read Paul, we have both more knowledge about science than he did *and* a broader perspective on his own writings and their audiences than he could ever have imagined. This gives us an advantage when reading Paul.

Those advantages give us the opportunity to evaluate Paul's writings in two ways. First, we can ask whether Paul might have written something different had he known what we know. How much of what Paul wrote was anchored to his time and place and his sense of an impending change to the cosmos, and how much of it might be more universally applicable? Second, we can ask whether interpretations of Paul's writings are fair or not—whether modern readings of Paul are evaluating him in full light of what we know about the limitations of his perspective. This might sound to some Christians as if we are picking and choosing what to believe about Paul's writings, but that's not really what we are doing at all. Responsible biblical interpretation requires that we take advantage of every tool that we have, and there's nothing truer or nobler about a so-called "plain" or "literal" reading of the text. Every interpretation is just that—an interpretation—and all interpretations come with their own biases and limitations. My bias and limitation is that I want my reading of Paul to include everything it can about his context and purpose, and I want to understand as much as I can about Paul's intentions before coming to a conclusion about his meaning.

A good basic question is whether Christian readings of Paul's teaching on sexuality have been fair. I think the answer is no. Conservative readings of Paul, such as those ensconced in the Christian purity movement, fail to account for Paul's eschatological worldview. They ignore the fact that his comments about sexuality were made when Paul was convinced that time was almost up. When we forget this about Paul, we distort Paul's meaning. He doesn't endorse singleness and celibacy because he thinks they're the best policy forever and always; he endorses singleness and celibacy because he thinks marriage and sex would be a distraction from the larger "impending crisis" of the end of the world. Likewise, his endorsement of marriage wasn't because he thought marriage itself was good for its own sake, although he might well have thought that if he had lived in different circumstances. Instead, he endorsed marriage because he thought it was a good way to contain unchecked sexual urges. When conservative Christians, such as those behind True Love Waits, point to "biblical marriage" using Paul's words from his letters, they are endorsing a worldview in which sex is a dangerous force in the world, and marriage is almost a necessary evil (or at least a necessary inconvenience) for containing it. They are endorsing a view of sex and marriage that comes out of a completely different context, and applying it to our own twenty-first–century world.

The truth is that Paul didn't contemplate the kind of world in which twenty-first–century conservative Christians live. He never imagined that the world would go on this long, or that Jesus' return would be so delayed. So, his view of human sexuality was never wide enough to encompass our world. Paul *might* have had some idea about romantic love and the human need for companionship beyond sex that marriage can provide, but, if he did, he didn't mention it, because his circumstances made his perspective very narrow. Paul's ideas about gentile sexual licentiousness don't make sense in a world in which virtually all Christians are gentiles, and where no serious person entertains the idea that different groups of people have different sexual drives that need controlling.[4] Any reading of Paul that lifts his writings out of the ancient world without taking account of these huge differences is bound to be a bad reading. True Love Waits and its ideological cousins are exactly that.

---

[4]Plenty of *un-serious* people entertain this idea, especially when espousing racist ideas about human nature, but I'm not going to cite them.

However, progressive Christians don't do a lot better. They constantly speculate about why Paul had so many sexual hang-ups. Was he repressed in some way? Did he hate women, or did he have some kind of Freudian issue with his mother or his father? Was he simply a misanthrope? However, the progressive instinct to hate Paul usually doesn't account for the simplest and most obvious explanation: he lived two thousand years ago, in a time before modern science, and everything we know about his ideas comes from letters that he didn't write to us, and which he never intended for us to read.

I don't think either conservative or progressive Christians read Paul very fairly. It's not true that he was setting a paradigm for love and marriage for all times and places, and likewise it's not true that he was a repressed prude. What *is* true is that both readings of Paul ignore important things about his motivations, his audience, his genre, and his worldview. I think that taking account of those things can lead us to an important conclusion: Paul was not a prude.

Paul and Modern Sexual Ethics

If a "plain" or "literal" reading of Paul's comments on sexuality is not a good one because it doesn't take account of his context, then what would a good reading look like? I think there are some ways we can read Paul's comments about sex and relationships responsibly, using the advantages we have in understanding his world and ours. When we read his writings this way, the Paul who emerges is not a prude, but an advocate of relationships that have integrity, justice, and love at the core. Reading Paul this way involves looking for the principles behind his writings rather than the specific recommendations, and when we undertake this kind of interpretation we are rewarded with a robust vision of human sexuality and relationships that can help us build a progressive sexual ethic that is just and liberative. Here are two of those principles.

First, Paul always views human sexuality and relationships through the lens of a sacred and vulnerable body. By this, I don't mean the same thing as "purity" advocates mean, as if any sexual activity will pollute one's pure body and contaminate one's soul. Instead, I mean that Paul understands that the body is a permeable thing that is prone to being wounded, abused, and damaged by misuse. Notice how often Paul talks about bodies in the context of community, as in 1 Corinthians 6, 11, and 12. He understands that bodies are a place where people can hurt each other deeply, and that great care needs to be taken with our own bodies and other people's bodies. For Paul, relationality is central to bodily ethics; nearly every time he talks about bodies, he does so in the context of relationships and communities.

This puts love at the center of sexual ethics. This is not just erotic love, although it is that. It is also about the care of persons and selves, and the way our relationships reflect our values. Paul thinks that bodies are a way for injury and pollution to gain access to people, which can sound like a very body-negative way of thinking. However, this view also reflects his observation that whole selves include bodies, and that what happens to our bodies is extremely important. This strikes me as a value that is very much in keeping with progressive Christianity; persons' souls matter, but their bodies matter too, and what happens to their bodies matters a lot. Any ethic that ignores the body or denigrates it is an ethic that fails to include whole persons.

Paul also believes that following Jesus should change the pattern of our lives. He means something profound by it. The long list of behaviors Paul recounts in 1 Corinthians, and the behaviors he rattles off in his vice lists, and his comments in 1 Thessalonians 4:3–8 and in similar places together show that his overriding ethic is that the fact of Jesus' life, death, and resurrection ought to have an effect on us. It ought to change who we are and how we relate to other people in the world. Some of this is Paul's knee-jerk reaction to what he sees as gentile immorality, but a lot of it is Paul's conviction that faith in Jesus (and the faithfulness *of* Jesus) ought to awaken us to new ways of being in relationship. When Paul argues against particular varieties or instances of sex, this is usually because he understands them to be unjust and degrading to one or more parties in the relationship. Paul thinks that, in light of Jesus, all of that should be left in the past.

A second principle we can draw from Paul's writings is that he was aware and affirming of a variety of ways of being an embodied being. Of course, Paul didn't live in our world, and he neither knew nor affirmed all the different expressions we can know and affirm. However, Paul does comment in 1 Corinthians about virgins, celibate people, long-time married folk, people who get married out of the need to express sexual urges, and widows. In all of these situations, Paul acknowledges that people in a variety of circumstances and with a variety of dispositions and urges can live holy and acceptable lives. There is no one-size-fits-all prescription from Paul (even though he does think it best, in light of the "impending crisis," to remain unmarried). Paul knows about and affirms lots of different ways of being. We can do the same, recognizing that one of Paul's core principles was an orientation toward Jesus and toward each other as fully human beings.

Paul thinks that relationships are expressions of the values of our faith, and that faith is always relational and never individual. Relationships, including sexual ones, are a way for us to know ourselves and a way for us to live in the world as social and communal beings.

Paul only objects to expressions of sexuality that violate relationships and hurt people, and he affirms (although sometimes reluctantly) sexual expressions that rightly put the integrity of persons at the center. Paul was not a prude. He was, from everything we know about him, unmarried and celibate, but he understood the importance of sexuality and relationships, and he affirmed those things when he saw them working for the good and not harming people. He had a very narrow understanding of where he lived in history—a wrong understanding, as we now know—and that caused him sometimes to discourage sex and marriage as unnecessary distractions. But, he affirmed human sexuality as an instrument of love and community, and he always insisted that what we do with our bodies ought to reflect respect for each other and ourselves, and that in all our actions we ought to be just. I think we can agree with him on that.

CHAPTER 6

Paul the Slavery Apologist

The Hermeneutic of "Hell No!"

Nancy Ambrose might be one of my favorite biblical interpreters, although many people have never heard of her. I myself have never met her, heard her speak, or read anything written by her. Most of what we know about her comes to us via her grandson, Howard Thurman, who was an important intellectual, author, and theologian. Thurman, in his book *Jesus and the Disinherited,* tells of how one of his boyhood "chores" was reading the Bible to his grandmother, who was not able to read for herself. "I was deeply impressed by the fact that she was most particular about the choice of Scripture," Thurman writes, and he goes on to relate the kinds of things she liked to hear. She liked to have Isaiah, the Psalms, and "the Gospels most of all," read to her, he said, but "the Pauline epistles never—except, at long intervals, the thirteenth chapter of First Corinthians."[1] Mrs. Ambrose had her reasons. She was born an enslaved person on a plantation in Florida, he wrote, and when he finally worked up the courage to ask her about her refusal to hear Paul's letters read to her, she replied:

> During the days of slavery, the master's minister would occasionally hold services for the slaves. Old man McGhee was so mean that he would not let a Negro minister preach to his slaves. Always the white minister used as his text something from Paul. At least three or four times a year he used as his text: "Slaves, be obedient to them that are your masters..., as unto Christ." Then he would go on to show how it was God's will that we were slaves and how, if we were good and happy slaves, God would bless us. I promised my Maker that if I ever

---

[1] Howard Thurman, *Jesus and the Disinherited* (Nashville: Abingdon-Cokesbury Press, 1949), 30.

learned to read and if freedom ever came, I would not read that part of the Bible.[2]

I once had a student call this "the hermeneutic of 'hell no,'" and I think that's a pretty great way to put it.[3] The first choice of any interpreter of texts is to decide which texts to read, and Mrs. Ambrose had a clear sense of how her hermeneutic worked: anything that had been used to try to keep her enslaved was a nonstarter for her. That meant that Paul was off the table. If Paul had been a friend of the master's minister, she reasoned, then Paul would not be a friend of hers. The exception was 1 Corinthians 13—the "love chapter"—which she would occasionally allow. But, for the most part, Paul's usefulness in the cause of slavery had made him useless to her.

The text cited by the master's minister in Ambrose's story was Ephesians 6:5–8, but it was not the only text attributed to Paul that found its way into the sermons of white antebellum slavery apologist preachers. First Corinthians 7:21–24; Colossians 3:22–25; Titus 2:9–10; 1 Timothy 6:1–2; Romans 13 (which we will examine more closely in the next chapter because of its use in current debates about immigration); and Paul's letter to Philemon were all used with regularity to bolster the cause of slavery, and they were all inflicted on enslaved persons in religious services meant to pacify them and convince them to be content with their earthly bondage.[4] Passages from the Hebrew Bible were used as well, but of all the biblical authors, none was of more use to pro-slavery preachers than Paul. Nancy Ambrose's animosity toward Paul was well-earned.

When talking to progressive Christian friends today, I hear a sentiment about Paul that's very similar to Nancy Ambrose's. Even granting that Paul lived in a different time and place, in which slavery was normal and unquestioned, my friends say that Paul's choice to reinforce the structures of slavery is unforgivable. Even in a world in which opposing slavery would have been unthinkable, they say, Paul could at least have remained neutral on the matter. Instead, he endorses the institution, and encourages enslaved people to think of their servitude as divinely ordained and not worth challenging or changing. How could this be the same person who confidently

---

[2] Ibid., 30–31.

[3] The student's name is Daryl Walker, and in addition to being a keen exegete, he is one of the most talented church musicians I have ever met.

[4] An excellent account of this kind of preaching, and the counter-exegesis undertaken by enslaved people, can be found in Emerson B. Powery and Rodney S. Sadler Jr., *The Genesis of Liberation: Biblical Interpretation in the Antebellum Narratives of the Enslaved* (Louisville: Westminster John Knox, 2016). They expertly trace the effects of the "master's minister" and connect the story of Nancy Ambrose to others who resisted the biblical interpretation of slaveholder religion.

proclaimed in Galatians 3:28 that "there is no longer slave or free?" How could this be the same Paul who gave his life to reaching gentiles, and leading them to the Jewish God? Slavery is today nearly universally acknowledged as an evil and ungodly institution, but, once upon a time, Christians defended and bolstered it using the words of Paul.

Seven texts written by or attributed to Paul figured prominently in the arguments of the slavery apologists. These texts cover a wide range of Paul's writings, from the core of his corpus in Romans and 1 Corinthians to his shortest letter in Philemon, and they include four of the pseudonymous texts that Paul likely did not write, but which bear his name. These seven texts all present different interpretive challenges, so I will consider them one by one (but will group the four pseudo-Paul writings together). Together, these passages have helped form the sense that Paul was a staunch defender of slavery, but when examined closely in light of modern biblical scholarship, these passages point us in a different direction—not to Paul as an abolitionist, opposing slavery, but neither as the friend to slavery that the preachers of slaveholding religion imagined him to be. When subjected to scrutiny, Paul's reputation as a supporter of slavery largely evaporates, leaving a much more complicated portrait of a person who worked within the confines and restrictions of his culture and age, trying to help win release for at least one enslaved person and encouraging other enslaved people to seek opportunity for their own release too. Much of the worst of what is attributed to Paul about slavery, Paul did not write, and what remains has been so often misused and misinterpreted that we have a completely unrepresentative picture of Paul's stance on slavery. With the help of modern biblical scholarship we can recover a Paul who is far from a slavery apologist, and who might even be an ally in the struggle for emancipation.

Pseudo-Paul on Slavery

Of all the biblical texts cited by the defenders of slavery, four stand out as the most important. These four texts were used more often than the rest, probably because their message is so clear—exactly the kind of message a proponent of slavery wanted to hear. Ephesians 6:5–8, Colossians 3:22–25, Titus 2:9, and 1 Timothy 6:1–2 were the favorite texts of the master's minister because of the forthrightness with which they presented the correctness of slavery. The Ephesians passage includes, "Slaves, obey your earthly masters with fear and trembling, in singleness of heart, as you obey Christ" (v. 5), and encourages enslaved people to "[r]ender service with enthusiasm, as to the Lord" (v. 7a). The

Colossians text essentially mirrors the same material, as large parts of Colossians and Ephesians do, and the 1 Timothy passage encourages enslaved people to "regard their masters as worthy of all honor," and asks people enslaved by fellow members of the church to "serve them all the more, since those who benefit by their service are believers and beloved." Titus says much the same. Together these verses are an unmistakable endorsement of slavery, and a clear attempt to make the Christian life identical with being an obedient slave. It was to this that Nancy Ambrose was objecting, and this is precisely what caused her to swear off most of Paul for the rest of her life.

What Nancy Ambrose could not have known was that Paul did not write any of those texts. Both Colossians and Ephesians belong to the "disputed" epistles that a majority of mainstream scholars believe Paul did not write, and 1 Timothy and Titus are two of the "Pastoral Epistles," which even many conservative Christian scholars no longer think Paul wrote. As I mentioned in the first chapter, in these letters the differences in style, vocabulary, and theme are too great for Paul plausibly to be the author. Most scholars have concluded that these letters belong to a second generation of people writing in Paul's name, trying to capitalize on his reputation and authority in order to advance their own agendas. This generation of pseudo-Paul authors has been extremely successful in this goal, as their frequent citations by pro-slavery preachers in the nineteenth century attest. They got exactly what they wanted, which was for their views to be cloaked in the authority of Paul's name and be spread far and wide.

As we have already seen in chapter 2, the agendas of the pseudo-Pauline authors included reinforcing a traditional social order. Writing some years into the Christian tradition, at a time when the church was trying to gain legitimacy in the eyes of their non-Christian neighbors, pseudo-Pauline authors (and other authors within the Christian tradition at the same time) often leaned into traditional Greek and Roman cultural norms, hoping to show how Christianity was not a threat to the social order. The particular sections of Colossians and Ephesians that include endorsements of slavery are often called the "household codes," because they have a strong interest in bolstering traditional and conservative notions of the household, including the subordination of women. These texts' agenda about slavery fits right in with that; these passages from Colossians and Ephesians are interested in maintaining traditional social order by encouraging enslaved people to accept their lot and serve happily.

This agenda—maintaining the social order—was exactly what pro-slavery preachers in the American South had in mind, too. They were defenders of the status quo, because they profited from the status quo, and perhaps also because of a sense of cultural traditionalism, which in their case was deeply aligned with racism born out of and married to their slaveholder Christianity. These preachers were not starting from the broad principles of the gospel as articulated by Jesus, because Jesus never said very much that a slavery advocate would find useful or amenable. Instead, they were seizing on texts from a later generation of Christian writers, who lived at a time when it made sense to cozy up to the power of the dominant social class.

There is some comfort in knowing that Paul did not write these texts from Ephesians, Colossians, Titus, and 1 Timothy, but the fact remains that *some* early Christian *did* write them. While we can exonerate Paul for these particular slavery-endorsing texts, we cannot exonerate early Christianity. Over the centuries, Christianity has tended to behave the way these pseudo-Pauline texts behave—to postpone questions of justice in order to accommodate itself better to the interests of power, or to maintain its own cultural, economic, and social power. There are usually ways to rationalize this: Christians have been able to convince themselves that justice can wait a little while longer, in the interest of expediency. Martin Luther King Jr. in his "Letter from a Birmingham Jail" condemned such fecklessness and meekness of white moderates, especially white moderate clergy, who urged patience—which was really inaction cloaked in a false virtue.[5] In my own career, I have seen the same dynamic play out with regard to LGBTQI inclusion; many people who claim to be allies have suggested slowing down the movement toward inclusion, or postponing it, to protect the sensibilities of those who might be offended. This is a time-honored tradition in the church, as "Christian" as communion and Easter, and progressive Christians must resist what King called the "do nothingism" of the moderate church.

The early church possessed the theological resources to critique slavery. As early as Paul, and in the pages of Colossians (3:11), the church knew the mantra: "There is no longer Jew or Greek, there is no longer slave or free, there is no longer male and female; for you are all one in Christ Jesus." (Gal. 3:28). That makes it even more disappointing that the early Christians who wrote Colossians, Ephesians, Titus, and 1 Timothy supported oppressors and told slaves to obey their masters. They *knew* better, but they did not *do* better. Their failure should be a lesson to us today.

---

[5]Martin Luther King Jr., "Letter from a Birmingham City Jail," April 16, 1963, pdf of original available at https://kinginstitute.stanford.edu/king-papers/documents/letter-birmingham-jail.

There is something *especially* toxic and bankrupt about these passages because all four of those letters go a step beyond encouraging enslaved people to serve their masters and be happy with their status. That would have been bad enough, but the authors of both Ephesians and Colossians go on to make another comparison or connection. Ephesians says to "obey your earthly masters with fear and trembling... as you obey Christ," and Colossians says to "obey your earthly masters in everything...fearing the Lord" (3:22). First Timothy, meanwhile, recommends obedience to masters "so that the name of God and the teaching may not be blasphemed" (6:1b). This is theological malpractice: equating obedience to humans with obedience to God, and making "the name of God and the teaching" equivalent with honoring unjust social structures. These are not, and cannot ever be, the same thing, as we will see in more detail in chapter 7. Augustine recognized this a few centuries later when he described the "earthly city" in relation to the "city of God"; the power structures of humans are separate from the spiritual realm, and it is a mistake to confuse them with each other.[6] Making obedience to *any* human the same thing as obedience to God is wrong, but it is *especially wrong* to make obedience to God equivalent to obedience to a slaveholder.

Nancy Ambrose saw through the Ephesians text, and presumably the Colossians, Titus, and 1 Timothy texts as well. Thinking that Paul had written them, she refused to hear Paul—she employed the "hermeneutic of 'hell no!'" But, before we move on to the other Pauline texts (the authentic ones) used to support slavery, I want to make one final point about these pseudo-Pauline texts and Nancy Ambrose's perspective on them. It's not quite true that she abandoned all association with Paul. As her grandson Howard Thurman points out, she would occasionally ("at long intervals") listen to Paul's discourse on love, found in 1 Corinthians 13. This tells me that although Nancy Ambrose was not a modern biblical scholar, she knew intuitively what many of those scholars have concluded, which is that the pro-slavery texts of Ephesians, Colossians, Titus, and 1 Timothy don't have much in common with the message of the person who wrote the "love chapter." Without the benefit of text criticism or historical criticism or any other tools of modern biblical scholarship, or even being able to read these texts for herself, Nancy Ambrose perceived the difference between the authentic Paul and pseudo-Paul, and with that distinction in mind, we turn to some of the texts on slavery that Paul *did* write.

---

[6]Augustine of Hippo, *City of God,* trans. Henry Bettenson (London: Penguin, 2003).

Paul on Slavery in 1 Corinthians

In the discussion on 1 Corinthians 7 in the previous chapter, and its pro-singleness and celibacy messages, we saw how Paul's unique eschatology influenced his writing in that chapter; Paul was convinced that he and the Corinthians were living very late in history, and that God was about to intervene in the world in the form of Jesus' second coming. Because of that, in 1 Corinthians 7 Paul was arguing for people to stay in their current situations unless they had a compelling reason not to, such as avoiding sin. He thought that time was so short that the only real reason to try to change your situation—the only reason to get married, for example, instead of staying single—was if you simply could not help yourself, and needed the structure of marriage to avoid committing the sin of fornication.

First Corinthians 7:21–24 comes right in the middle of that discourse, and as it is translated in the NRSV, Paul's argument there relies on the same sense of impending crisis. "Were you a slave when called? Do not be concerned about it," Paul writes in the NRSV. "Even if you can gain your freedom, make use of your present condition now more than ever." Paul goes on to clarify the implications of this: "For whoever was called in the Lord as a slave is a freed person belonging to the Lord, just as whoever was free when called is a slave of Christ" (vv.21–22). There is a simple argument to be made about this text, which is parallel to the argument I made in the previous chapter about marriage relationships. Paul is simply not concerned about anyone's specific social situation or status, because he believes the end is coming so soon that any temporary conditions are irrelevant in the long term. If Paul had known that the world would go on for nineteen more centuries and counting, he might have given different advice, but his sense of urgency about the eschaton impelled him to advise enslaved people: "Do not be concerned about it." Even on the basis of the NRSV translation, there is reason to see this passage as less than a full-fledged endorsement of slavery. It is, in its most pro-slavery interpretation, a sign that Paul was willing to live with the status quo for a few more weeks, months, or years, until Jesus returned.

Yet the NRSV is papering over some difficulties in the Greek text of verse 21. The NRSV translates it as, "Were you a slave when called? Do not be concerned about it. Even if you can gain your freedom, make use of your present condition now more than ever." However, this might be an overconfident translation, because it supplies a few words in English that aren't there in the Greek. Because she can explain it better than I can, I'll let Shira Lander, the author of the notes to 1 Corinthians in *The Jewish Annotated New Testament,* say what the issues are here: "According to the NRSV translation, slaves should make the best of their current status, but Paul may be encouraging them to *make use of* the opportunity for emancipation *if* available to them."[7] This is probably the only time you'll ever see me say this, but *The Message* might have a better version of this verse than the NRSV: "If you have a chance at freedom, go ahead and take it." The NIV has something similar: "[I]f you can gain your freedom, do so." The conditional "even if" of the NRSV suggests the futility of trying to become free, in a way that fits with Paul's eschatology. In the NRSV, Paul is saying that freedom from slavery is neither here nor there when time is so short. However, the Greek is ambiguous in a way that might mean that a better reading of this sentence is that Paul sees the inherent value of freedom, and if the opportunity arises for an enslaved person to seek freedom, they should seize it.

As we will see, the reading by the NIV and *The Message* might fit in with Paul's attitude toward slavery in another of his writings, his letter to Philemon. In that letter, Paul avoids taking a direct stance on the moral rightness or wrongness of slavery, but he *might* be using his influence to pull some strings to try to win the freedom of an enslaved person, depending on how you read the letter. Meanwhile, here in 1 Corinthians, Paul seems to be tempering feelings about the importance of *any* social status or condition when the end is so near, but simultaneously acknowledging that there is value in freedom for freedom's sake. In fact, some enslaved persons in the American South pointed to this verse as it appeared in the *King James Version*—"if thou mayest be free, use it rather"—as a text of emancipation.[8] If Paul's alleged words could be used by the master's minister for oppression, it seems he could also be summoned to the side of the enslaved person searching for freedom.

Paul on Slavery in Philemon

Philemon is certainly Paul's strangest and most enigmatic letter. It is his shortest, at only 25 verses, and it is the only one of his letters that was written to an individual, not a community—although it is a kind of open letter, also addressed to two other people and meant to be read by others besides Philemon. Paul wrote the letter while imprisoned, and sent it to a man named Philemon, who probably lived in Colossae in Asia Minor. The subject of the letter is the fate of a man named Onesimus—"Useful," in Greek, the kind of name that was sometimes

---

[7]Shira Lander, "Notes on 1 Corinthians," in *The Jewish Annotated New Testament,* 2d ed. (Oxford: Oxford University Press, 2017), 334–35. Emphasis in the original.

[8]Powery and Sadler, *The Genesis of Liberation,* 168.

given to enslaved people—who had found Paul in prison and appealed to him to intervene on his behalf with Philemon.

The relationship between the two men is not clear. Traditionally, Onesimus was presumed to be Philemon's slave, on the basis of verses 15 and 16, which ask Philemon to welcome Onesimus "back forever, no longer as a slave but more than a slave, a beloved brother..." In that scenario, Onesimus had perhaps run away from his master Philemon and sought out the protection of Paul, someone he knew from Paul's time doing missionary work in Colossae. If this was the case, Onesimus was likely hoping to take advantage of a practice called *amicus domini,* a Latin phrase meaning "friend of the master," in which a fugitive slave could ask for help, protection, and mediation from someone who was the master's equal. Onesimus might have been counting on the status of Paul, who had evangelized Philemon, protecting him from Philemon and his wrath.

This is not the only possible interpretation, though. The reference in verse 16 is the only allusion to slavery in the letter, and it is not certain that it refers to a legal status of Onesimus. Paul routinely used the Greek word *doulos,* which could mean "servant" or "slave," in a theological sense, to describe the relationship between people (including himself) and Jesus, or between people and some other power, such as sin. It's possible that in Philemon 16, Paul was just using it in this sense, to say that Onesimus had turned away from a life of service to sin (or something else), and that Philemon should now think of him as a brother. Some interpreters think that Philemon and Onesimus were literally biologically brothers,[9] and had been estranged from one another, perhaps because Philemon had been evangelized by Paul but Onesimus had continued in his sinful ways, or something like that. Read this way, Paul's letter to Philemon is an announcement that Onesimus had changed his ways, and a plea for Philemon to accept his estranged brother as family once again.

We might never know the truth behind the composition of this letter. But, we *can* know how this letter has functioned in history. Following the passage of the Fugitive Slave Act of 1850, many defenders of the law pointed to Paul's letter to Philemon as scriptural justification of it. That law required anyone who encountered an escaped enslaved person—even someone in a state where slavery was not practiced—to return that person to slavery. The law criminalized the act of providing help and sanctuary to escaped slaves. If one reads the letter to Philemon as the plight of an escaped slave who appealed to Paul to intervene with the man who claimed to own him, then the letter takes

---

[9]Allen Dwight Callahan, *Embassy of Onesimus: The Letter of Paul to Philemon* (Valley Forge: Trinity, 1997).

on parallels to the scenario envisioned by the Fugitive Slave Act. In the letter, Paul sends Onesimus back to Philemon with a thinly veiled demand: "I am appealing to you for my child, Onesimus, whose father I have become during my imprisonment" (v. 10). Paul then goes on to make a pun out of the meaning of Onesimus' name: "Formerly he was useless to you, but now he is indeed useful both to you and to me. I am sending him, that is, my own heart, back to you" (vv. 11–12). Paul goes on to insinuate that Philemon, in turn, might send Onesimus back to Paul voluntarily, releasing him from service either permanently or temporarily.

For advocates of the Fugitive Slave Act, Paul's act of sending Onesimus back was scriptural backing for their position. If Paul sent Onesimus back into slavery, why should someone in Ohio or Maryland do any differently? People who defended slavery and the Fugitive Slave Act saw Paul's actions in the letter to Philemon as an example of the right thing to do: Paul sent Philemon's property back to him, just as a dutiful citizen would do and should do. Paul had set an example, the Act's defenders said, and everyone needed to follow it and enforce the Fugitive Slave Act as the law of the land and the will of God.

Yet even assuming that the letter to Philemon is describing a fugitive slave who is being sent back to his master, the letter is not a very good scriptural warrant for the Act. That's because in the letter Paul was not meekly deferring to the slaveholder's supposed authority over the enslaved and sending his property back to him; he was using his own power and authority to intervene with Philemon on Onesimus' behalf, and he was making Philemon an offer that he probably could not have refused: sending Onesimus back with a letter in which he used all of his power and authority on Onesimus' behalf.

For the first half of the letter, Paul is very deferential to Philemon, and very "genteel." He includes the usual greetings and pleasantries. But, beginning in verse 13, Paul springs the trap he has laid. "I wanted to keep him with me," Paul says of Onesimus, "but I preferred to do nothing without your consent, in order that your good deed might be voluntary and not something forced." Later on, Paul lays it on thick: "So if you consider me your partner, welcome him as you would welcome me" (v. 17). Paul personally offers to pay back any debts Onesimus has incurred, noting, "I, Paul, am writing this with my own hand: I will repay it. I say nothing about your owing me even your own self" (v. 19). Of course, by saying that he will say *nothing* about Philemon owing Paul his very life, Paul has said *everything*. He has put Philemon in an impossible position. Remember, this was an open letter, addressed to Philemon but also to two other named individuals "and the church in your house"

(v. 1d), or the congregation of worshiping Christians that was meeting in Philemon's house, with Philemon acting as a kind of patron-leader. In front of the whole church, Paul had asked for a favor that could not be denied. "Confident of your obedience," Paul writes, "I am writing to you, knowing that you will do even more than I say" (v. 21).

With these words, Paul is playing in the powerful streams of obligation, honor, and influence that flowed across Roman society. Every person in the Empire held a status and position with regard to other people. Almost everyone was someone else's inferior, and almost everyone was someone's superior. Relationships of patronage and service were a part of everyday life, and it seems that Paul felt as if he was Philemon's patron in certain ways—enough that he could pull Philemon's strings and feel confident that Philemon would do what he asked. He did this in full view of the community, knowing that if Philemon refused, he would be revealed as a violator of his social obligations and known as someone who turned down Paul's request—Paul, to whom Philemon owed his very self.

This is quite the power play on Paul's part, and he wouldn't have made it if he weren't fairly certain what the outcome would be. The icing on the cake comes in verse 22: "[P]repare a guest room for me," Paul asks, putting into play the possibility that he will drop by unannounced. The subtext is clear: "Do what I say, and if anything bad happens to Onesimus, I will be there soon to see it."

It's important to be clear what Paul is and is not doing in this letter. He is *not* asking for Philemon to emancipate Onesimus completely. In fact, he might be asking for something such as a transfer of ownership, although his language is vague. And Paul is certainly *not* taking a principled stand against slavery. He doesn't argue that slavery is wrong, or that Philemon has a moral obligation to release Onesimus and any other people he has enslaved. We wish that Paul had made those arguments, but he didn't, either because he didn't want to, or because they simply weren't conceptually available to him. In a world in which slavery was absolutely normal and common, it might never have occurred to Paul to tell Philemon that slavery as an institution and a practice was morally wrong.

But (assuming the scenario in which Onesimus is a runaway, and not Philemon's biological brother) Paul *was* throwing his weight around on behalf of a fugitive slave, and that's important. It reveals the use of the letter by defenders of the Fugitive Slave Act of 1850 as cynical and dishonest; they were claiming that Paul dutifully sent a slave back to his owner, when in fact Paul only did that as a way of actively intervening on behalf of a slave's well-being and at least relative freedom. Although defenders of the Act were citing Paul's letter to Philemon as evidence for their position, it was really closer to evidence *against* their position. Paul was intervening between an enslaved person and a slaveholder, on the side of the enslaved person, to deprive the slaveholder of what he considered his rightful property. He was giving aid and comfort to a runaway slave in the same way that violators of the Fugitive Slave Act were.

Paul and Civic Authority

Defenders of the Fugitive Slave Act and other such laws in the antebellum American South sometimes used another part of Paul's writings in their arguments: Romans 13. We will spend a lot more time with Romans 13 in the next chapter about immigration, including deeper discussion of how that chapter has been interpreted by people in various kinds of power, but there is a history with Romans 13 and the American practice of slavery.[10] In the October 30 1850 issue of the *Weekly North Carolina Standard,* a newspaper based in Raleigh, North Carolina (my native state), an article railed against Northern Congregationalist Christians.[11] Those Congregationalists had passed resolutions objecting to the Fugitive Slave Act, and they refused to follow the new law. The Raleigh newspaper lashed out at them, decrying their biblical interpretation, and offering some passages in rebuttal. One of those was Ephesians 6:5, telling slaves to obey their earthly masters. But the bulk of the argument came from Romans 13:

> These *Christians* in the free States set up their judgements against that of the Almighty, and blindly strike against all law, order, and right! Let them hear the language of St. Paul, as he invokes the Divine vengeance upon their evil deeds... We verily believe that the Abolition Ministers of the free States have done more harm in this matter, than the whole Northern population besides... [I]nstead of subjecting themselves unto the higher powers, they are advising sedition and insurrection."[12]

This newspaper article was written by practitioners of slavery, defending slavery on the basis of its legality. Because the Fugitive Slave Act was the law of the land, they reasoned, and the Congregationalist

---

[10]For a brief history of the use of Romans 13 in debates about the Fugitive Slave Act, see Lincoln Mullen, "The Fight to Define Romans 13," *The Atlantic,* June 15, 2018, accessed at https://www.theatlantic.com/ideas/archive/2018/06/romans-13/562916/. I am grateful to Mullen for pointing me to the October 30, 1950, edition of the *Weekly North Carolina Standard,* cited below.

[11]"The Fugitive Slave Law," *Weekly North Carolina Standard,* October 30, 1850.

[12]Ibid., 2. Emphases in the original.

ministers in the North were refusing to follow that law, they were subverting rightful authority in exactly the way Paul warned against in Romans 13. Elsewhere in the article, they also pointed to parts of the Hebrew Bible that assumed slavery, and they explained away similar passages that seemed to go against their position. Because Paul had said in Romans 13 that people should subject themselves to ruling authorities, or, as the newspaper quoted the *King James Version,* "Whoever therefore resisteth the power, resisteth the ordinance of God: and they that resist shall receive to themselves damnation" (v. 2). With these words, slaveholders reasoned that the abolitionist resisters of the Fugitive Slave Act were on the wrong side of God. Those Northern Congregationalists had set themselves against God, because they had opposed a rightful law of the land. The Congregationalists, for their part, reached a different interpretation of Romans 13, as shown in the resolutions of the New York Evangelical Congregational Association meeting that the Raleigh newspaper was condemning. Here they are as reported to an anti-slavery group in Massachusetts:

> *Resolved,* That while we recognize the obligation to obey the laws of the land, we make an exception in the case of all such provisions as contravene the "higher law" of God.

> *Resolved,* That we advise all persons to render every needful aid and comfort to Fugitive Slaves, just the same as if there were no law in the land forbidding it.[13]

This was a classic conflict in the period, and, as we will see in the next chapter, in other periods as well. On the one hand, those with civil authority on their side insisted that Paul meant to say in Romans 13 that all civil authority should be obeyed, always. On the other hand, others interpreted Paul's words in a more limited way, and pointed out that no civil law could overrule the "higher law" of God. In the next chapter, we will see that neither of these positions quite captures the meaning behind Paul's words in Romans 13, and that modern biblical scholarship has offered some intriguing new interpretations, but for now it's good to notice that while Paul was being used by the advocates of slavery, he was also being read and interpreted by its opponents. Paul was not only wielded as a weapon by the pro-slavery faction, he was also used by opponents of slavery, and by enslaved persons themselves, to argue against the institution.

---

[13]Massachusetts Anti-Slavery Society, *Annual Report Presented to the Massachusetts Anti-Slavery Society by Its Board of Managers* (Massachusetts Anti-Slavery Society, 1851), 71. Emphases in original.

Paul the Slavery Apologist?

Nancy Ambrose was justified in her rejection of Paul and his writings because a great deal of harm had been done to her and her people in Paul's name. My intention is not to minimize or second-guess that harm, but to point out that the harm done in Paul's name was only possible because people distorted, misrepresented, and misused Paul's writings. It was not Paul's writings that were to blame, or Paul himself, but it was the misuse of Paul, both deliberate and accidental, that contributed to the suffering of Nancy Ambrose and so many others like her. In the case of slavery, as in the other cases we have already seen in this book, Paul's bad reputation has not been deserved.

To begin with, the texts most commonly cited to show Paul's supposed support for slavery likely don't come from Paul at all. Ephesians, Colossians, Titus, and 1 Timothy are all pseudo-Pauline texts, written after Paul's death to capitalize on his reputation and authority. As was the case in this book's chapter discussing misogyny, the inclusion of pro-slavery statements in the pseudo-Pauline literature might even be evidence that later writers considered Paul's stance on slavery to need "correction." At the very least, those later writers thought that Paul's stance on slavery was too vague or mild. These pseudo-Pauline texts exist not because Paul *was* a slavery apologist, but because he was *not* one, so slavery apologists appropriated his name to their cause.

Now, 1 Corinthians, which certainly *was* written by Paul, *seems* to show that Paul supported slavery, or at least considered it not to be a very big deal. "Were you a slave when called?" Paul asked. "Do not be concerned about it" (7:21a). This is the kind of thing that only someone who was *not* enslaved could have said. But here we have to keep Paul's eschatological expectation in mind. He expected Jesus' return at any time, and so he was not very concerned with changing unjust or unhappy circumstances, because all circumstances were temporary. Furthermore, as we saw, the second half of verse 21 is best interpreted as Paul encouraging enslaved persons to seek freedom if they could. First Corinthians 7, the only portion of Paul's authentic writings to address the issue of slavery directly, has an ambiguous and possibly even slightly pro-liberation meaning.

Defenders of slavery have used Paul's short letter to Philemon to support their cause, but their use of the letter is misguided. They point to the fact that Paul sent the slave Onesimus back to Philemon, but if Onesimus was in fact an escaped slave (and not Philemon's brother), Paul's letter hardly counts as support for their position. In the letter, Paul was using the full weight of his apostolic and pastoral authority on behalf of Onesimus, strong-arming Philemon into releasing him—either releasing him into Paul's service or completely manumitting him. We wish Paul had made different arguments in Philemon, such as an argument about the moral wrongness of slavery, but he was working within the systems he had at his disposal to do the most he could do for Onesimus.

There will be much more to say about Romans 13 in the next chapter, but already we have seen how easy it was for the Northern abolitionists to puncture the Southern slaveholders' arguments about it. Romans 13 is probably not actually about the kind of civil authority the defenders of slavery had in mind anyway, but even if it's read that way, it's easy to subvert human laws to the superiority of God's law. Paul's words in Romans 13 are the thinnest of justifications for slavery, and those justifications come from later interpreters, not from Paul himself.

What, then, can we say about Paul and slavery? I am confident in saying that Paul was not a slavery apologist, but he was also a person who lived in a time when slavery was normal. I don't know that it occurred to Paul to challenge the broader systems that made slavery possible. He eroded the system around the edges, as with his intervention on behalf of Onesimus, and even in pseudo-Pauline books there are instructions to slaveholders to treat their slaves kindly (as if that made the practice better or most just).[14]

One the things that bothers me most about Paul's writings is his consistent use of the word *doulos* to make theological points. *Doulos,* as noted earlier, means "servant" or "slave," and Paul used it frequently when he wanted to talk about devotion or obligation. He called himself a *doulos* of Jesus Christ (Rom. 1:1; Gal. 1:10; Phil. 1:1), he talks about being "slaves of sin" (Rom. 6:20), and he presents the idea of being "slaves to righteousness" as something to be attained (Rom. 6:19). The way Paul uses the word, it's clear that he thinks being a slave is bad, unless you're a slave to something in the sense of being completely devoted to it, and he seems to think that being free is good. Paul assumes that a certain amount of devotion should be expected to flow from slaves to slaveholders. This tells me that he presumed the system and presumed its normality enough to use it to make metaphors, even if he didn't presume its morality. It's a subtle thing, but the way he used the word *doulos* tells me that Paul probably did not actively question the institution of slavery. He assumed that it was part of life, and that it was something to be avoided and even opposed, but that it was inevitable.

---

[14]Ephesians 6:9; Colossians 4:1.

Nancy Ambrose was not completely wrong about Paul. Her suspicions were well-founded. Because she refused to hear most of Paul's writings, but agreed ("at long intervals") to hear 1 Corinthians 13, it seems that Nancy Ambrose was able to discern between Paul's most authentic writings and pseudo-Pauline material that had been falsely attributed to him. She could see the value in his poetic reflections on love in 1 Corinthians, even as she rejected the words in Ephesians, Colossians, Titus, and 1 Timothy that were levied against her by the master's ministers. Nancy Ambrose had a hermeneutic of Paul that is strikingly modern, and we would do well to follow her lead, and listen most closely to Paul when he talks about love and inclusion.

CHAPTER 7

Paul the Xenophobe

Paul and the Attorney General

It's actually not that easy to arrive at an opinion that "Paul is a xenophobe." There's nothing in Paul's writings that really lends itself to a statement such as that, and not even the pseudo-Pauline material deals with questions about foreigners, immigration, and the like. The closest you could get is that persistent bias that Paul had—which we've been talking about all through the book—that gentiles were of a different character than Jews. Paul thought that gentiles were especially susceptible to temptation and prone to sinful activities. But he also devoted his life to *reaching* gentiles, so that bias didn't totally dominate his views.

As a Jewish person living and traveling throughout the eastern Roman Empire, Paul would have encountered lots of stereotypes aimed at *him*. His use of the name Paul instead of his given name Saul is a clue that, as was the case for most imperial subjects and members of colonized groups, Paul needed to negotiate his identity constantly in a way that would make him seem less strange or dangerous to the people he met, and that would keep him out of trouble. Sometimes, Paul was better at staying out of trouble than at other times (he was never *very* good at it), but he knew when he was a stranger in town and how to mitigate the effects of that. He had his biases, and others undoubtedly had biases about him, but overall Paul avoided the questions of xenophobia, migration, and immigration in his letters.

However, recent events in the United States have dragged Paul into an ongoing debate about immigration. In the spring and summer of 2018, controversy exploded over immigration policies being instituted and enforced at the southern border with Mexico and throughout the country. Under the administration of Donald Trump, Immigration and Customs Enforcement (or ICE, part of the Department of Homeland

Security) began targeting people for deportation, aggressively prosecuting offenses that previously would have been low priorities, shifting resources to immigration enforcement, and, most sinisterly, separating parents from their children and incarcerating each in different facilities without the possibility of seeing one another or, in many cases, knowing anything about each other's safety or whereabouts. In my opinion, this is one of the great national shames in recent history. But, this not a book about immigration policy. It is a book about Paul and the ways he has been interpreted, and so I had not expected to include a chapter in it about immigration. I didn't include it in the proposal I wrote, or in the first drafts of the book, but one day I saw something on the news that made me email Chalice Press and ask them if I could add this chapter at the last minute: I saw United States Attorney General at the time, Jeff Sessions, citing Paul to defend his immigration policy. And, I knew I had to write another chapter.

"I would cite you to [*sic*] the Apostle Paul and his clear and wise command in Romans 13," Sessions said in a speech, "to obey the laws of the government because God has ordained them for his purposes." Sessions went on: "Orderly and lawful processes are good in themselves, and protect the weak and lawful." Asked about this later on, Sarah Huckabee Sanders, White House Press Secretary, expressed a similar opinion: "It is very biblical to enforce the law."[1] Of course, any citizen of a *secular* democracy might immediately object and ask why the book of Romans should be cited as the basis of for an immigration policy or law enforcement generally, and they would be justified in doing so. But, this is not a book about political science, either.

No, this is a book about Paul, and as I read their comments and watched the tape, I was struck by the way Sanders and especially Sessions were using Paul. Both of them, but especially Sessions, seemed to think that it was completely self-evident that Paul's comments in Romans 13 made the question of compliance with laws an open-and-shut matter. "Orderly and lawful processes are good in themselves" is a pretty confident statement—a statement that could only be made by someone who has never been systematically discriminated against by the law itself. Sessions is, as am I, a white man from the South, so I hope he will forgive me for assuming that our experiences are similar. I know that the law treats me differently than it treats other people, by virtue of my skin and my gender (and my sexuality and my economic class and my level of education and my citizenship status, to name

[1] Emily McFarlan Miller and Yonat Shimron, "Why Is Jeff Sessions Quoting Romans 13 and Why Is the Bible Verse So Often Invoked?," *USA Today*, accessed September 14, 2018, https://www.usatoday. com/story/news/2018/06/16/jeff-sessions-bible-romans-13-trump-immigration-policy/707749002/.

but a few other factors). I'm under no illusions that the law is some benevolent and all-good entity that doesn't care who you are. Both the law and those who enforce the law have biases.

Where does Paul fit into this, as a Jewish person operating in the Roman Empire, writing a letter to the churches in the Empire's capital city of Rome? Was Paul more like me and Sessions, with an uncomplicated relationship with the law and law enforcement that was enabled by layers of privilege? Or, was Paul more like the undocumented parents and children swept up in raids and separated at the border? Perhaps it's best to let Paul say it for himself:

> Are they ministers of Christ? I am talking like a madman—I am a better one: with far greater labors, far more imprisonments, with countless floggings, and often near death. Five times I have received from the Jews the forty lashes minus one.[2] Three times I was beaten with rods.[3] Once I received a stoning. Three times I was shipwrecked; for a night and a day I was adrift at sea; on frequent journeys, in danger from rivers, danger from bandits, danger from my own people, danger from gentiles, danger in the city, danger in the wilderness, danger at sea, danger from false brothers and sisters; in toil and hardship, through many a sleepless night, hungry and thirsty, often without food, cold and naked... In Damascus, the governor under King Aretas guarded the city of Damascus in order to seize me, but I was let down in a basket through a window in the wall, and escaped from his hands.
>
> (2 Cor. 11:23–27, 32–33)

Paul had much more in common with someone sitting in an ICE detention facility than he had in common with me or Jeff Sessions. That has to be the starting point for interpreting his letter to the Christians in Rome, and especially for a section such as chapter 13 in which he seems to have so much to say about civil authority and government. Sessions' and Sanders' comments make Paul's words in Romans 13 into an uncomplicated endorsement of government and civil power, as if Paul had never had occasion to sit in a jail cell and contemplate the fairness of the law. But, Paul *was* imprisoned at least two or three times (he brags about "far more imprisonments" in 2 Corinthians 11:23, so the real number is likely higher), and his tone does not suggest that

---

[2] A punishment described in Deuteronomy 25:1–3, resulting from losing a court case.

[3] This is probably a punishment given out by Roman officials, not Jewish ones, according to Alan J. Avery-Peck, "Notes on The Second Letter of Paul to the Corinthians," in *The Jewish Annotated New Testament*, 2d ed. (Oxford: Oxford, 2017), 369.

he thought all of his run-ins with the law were well-deserved. Nor, as we will see, do his comments in the letter to the Romans itself support a law-and-order Paul. Paul spent a lot of his life slipping through borders and over walls, facing punishment from officials who didn't understand him, tolerating unjust prison sentences, and staying one step ahead of mobs, soldiers, and death. In all likelihood, death finally caught up with Paul at the hands of the emperor in Rome. That doesn't square with someone who can say "Let every person be subject to the governing authorities; for there is no authority except from God, and those authorities that exist have been instituted by God" (Rom. 13:1), and mean it in any uncomplicated way. No, Paul's words in Romans demand interpretation, and, as it turns out, ever since they were written down people on every side of power have been reading and interpreting them. Unsurprisingly, people in power, such as Jeff Sessions, tend to read Paul's words as a plain call to obey governments. Meanwhile, people on the *underside* of power, such as Paul in his Philippian prison cell and Pablo in his ICE facility—separated from his kids—have read it very differently.

Romans 13 in Context

Before we launch into different ways Romans 13 has been interpreted over the years, it's important to take a step back and look at what that chapter actually says, and how it fits into the rest of the letter to the Romans.

This section comes relatively late in the letter to the Romans, only a few chapters before the end and after many long chapters of dense discourse. Romans is not like Paul's other letters, because he was writing it to people he did not know and who did not owe him anything. In Romans, there's no hint of the Paul who could push Philemon around to get his way, or the Paul of 1 Corinthians who chastised his congregation for various misdeeds. In Romans, Paul is deferential. Only a few verses into the letter, Paul catches himself preparing to promise to teach and guide them, and instead qualifies his authority: "For I am longing to see you so that I may share with you some spiritual gift to strengthen you— or rather so that we may be mutually encouraged by each other's faith, both yours and mine" (Rom. 1:11–12). When talking to the Romans, Paul is aware that they don't owe him anything, that his authority with them is by reputation only, and that his reputation might actually make them *less* interested in hearing from him. He treads carefully. He allows that he might learn a thing or two from them, too.

The New Perspective on Paul has helped to show how much of the letter to the Romans is about the question of how Jews and gentiles fit together with the same God. As we will see in the next chapter, for centuries this book has been read as if it is a theological textbook or an essay on salvation, but that's not really what it's about at all. This becomes clearer when the letter is viewed through the New Perspective, and especially the Radical New Perspective. For most of Romans, leading up to chapter 13, Paul has been wrestling with various aspects of the relationship between Jews and gentiles in the church. He must have thought that Jewish-gentile relations were a big problem in the churches in Rome, and there are historical reasons to think this might have been true. Rome had a large Jewish population and at least several synagogues in the first century, and in the 49 c.e. the emperor Claudius seems to have expelled all Jews from the city temporarily as a punishment. This might well have led to tension or conflict between Jewish and gentile members of churches—a situation in which the Jews, who were there first, had been expelled and then replaced in the church structure by gentiles. When the Jews returned to town years later, there definitely could have been disagreement over how things ought to be. That might be the reason Paul spent so much time in Romans going over the relative status of Jews and gentiles.[4]

We will look more closely at all of that in the next chapter, but for now it's enough to know that Paul had been focused on this issue for most of the letter up to chapter 13. He had been carefully sifting through questions of Jewish precedence and gentile pride, trying to find a way to speak to his presumed audience in Rome that would make him defuse any hard feelings they might have had about him, and predispose them to welcome him when he arrived in their city. By the time we get to Romans 13, he is nearing the end of these efforts; the letter only goes on for a few chapters more. Furthermore, all of chapter 16 is given over to greetings, and part of chapter 15 is about Paul's travel plans and his plea for help with his missionary plans, so really chapter 13 is one of the last big sections of content. That's why so many interpreters are surprised about what Paul does in Romans 13—he seems to change gears suddenly and begin talking about something new, and something that contrasted with some of the things he had just been saying earlier in the letter. Whereas he had spent a great deal of time and energy earlier in the letter talking about Jews and gentiles, Abraham and his inheritance, and the like, in chapter 13 Paul suddenly begins talking about something different:

---

[4]Not all scholars see this as the background of the situation in Rome. Some scholars, even those sympathetic to the New Perspective, think the audience of the letter has been oversimplified. Stanley K. Stowers, *A Rereading of Romans: Justice, Jews, and Gentiles* (New Haven, Conn.: Yale University, 1994), 22–39.

Let every person be subject to the governing authorities; for there is no authority except from God, and those authorities that exist have been instituted by God. Therefore whoever resists authority resists what God has appointed, and those who resist will incur judgement. For rulers are not a terror to good conduct, but to bad. Do you wish to have no fear of the authority? Then do what is good, and you will receive its approval; for it is God's servant for your good. But if you do what is wrong, you should be afraid, for the authority does not bear the sword in vain! It is the servant of God to execute wrath on the wrongdoer. Therefore one must be subject, not only because of wrath but also because of conscience. For the same reason you also pay taxes, for the authorities are God's servants, busy with this very thing. Pay to all what is due them—taxes to whom taxes are due, revenue to whom revenue is due, respect to whom respect is due, honor to whom honor is due.
(Rom. 13:1–7)

Why does Paul do this, and what does it mean? For centuries, interpreters have tried to figure out what prompted Paul to include this section, and what he might have meant by it. Very often, people in power have said that the meaning is obvious: Paul wants people to obey power, because power rightfully comes from God and serves the good. This is the position Jeff Sessions was citing when he defended U.S. immigration policy with Romans 13. Others, though, have looked for alternative explanations for the passage, and have read very different interpretations in Paul's words. We'll look at some of those interpretations now.

Origen of Alexandria on Romans 13

Origen was a Christian theologian, exegete, and scholar who lived at the end of the second century and the beginning and middle of the third century. He is one of the most important interpreters of the Bible ever to have lived, in part because he was alive at a time when the Christian tradition was still hammering out which texts would be authoritative, and how they should be interpreted. One of the hallmarks of Origen's scriptural interpretation was that he thought that a surface-level reading of scripture was the least-good way to read it. Reading scripture and asking what it meant on a literal level was alright for the simplest Christians, he thought, but we should always strive to look for the deeper meanings. Origen had a knack for finding meanings in even the most mundane of details—numbers, single words, geographical markers, and the like. But the plain meaning was almost never interesting to him.

In the case of Romans 13, Origen made something of an exception. In interpreting this passage, Origen stopped his usual deep-digging in scripture and poked his head above ground, and for a moment he considered the plain meaning of the text. Perhaps Origen was prompted to do so because of the subject matter of this particular passage. As a teenager, Origen's father was arrested and executed by the Roman Empire for practicing Christianity, and Origen reportedly wanted to get arrested as well, but he was prevented from doing so by his mother. He lived through periods of sporadic persecution, and as an old man Origen was caught up in the Decian persecution, the first empire-wide and systematic crackdown on Christians, beginning in the year 250.[5] Origen had spent most of his life on the wrong side of the civil authorities, and he was troubled by what he saw in Romans 13. Could Paul really mean what he said about civil authorities?

Origen turned this into an opportunity to demonstrate the way the surface meaning of the text is usually the worst meaning. If one were to read Romans 13 plainly and literally, one would come away with a view of civil authority as God-given and unquestionably good. Origen's own life had taught him differently, so he found different meanings in the text. About 13:2, which says that anyone resisting authority resists God, Origen writes, "Here he is not speaking about those authorities that instigate persecutions against the faith."[6] About verse 3, which suggests that good conduct will lead to the approval of authorities, Origen is incredulous: "Paul troubles [me] by these words," he writes, and he goes on to say that he has never heard of civil authorities giving approval for good conduct, only punishment for bad. "For there is no tradition for secular authorities to praise those who fail to become criminals," Origen writes, and he knows that there must be some other meaning at work in Paul's words. Origen's answer is that "Paul, even when he appears to be teaching about moral matters, always refuses to bypass the opportunity to insert something about the mysteries." Paul was actually talking about how all humans live under the shadow of sin, Origen wrote, and how when we are judged we will receive praise from God for the righteousness we live out in our lives.[7]

Origen is certain that the plain meaning of Paul's words cannot be the correct meaning. For him, it's obvious that Paul meant something

---

[5]John Anthony McGuckin, ed., *The Westminster Handbook to Origen*, The Westminster Handbooks to Christian Theology (Louisville: Westminster John Knox, 2004), 1–23.

[6]Origen, *Commentary on the Epistle to the Romans, Books 6—10*, trans. Thomas P. Scheck (Washington, D.C.: Catholic University of America Press, 2002), 223.

[7]Ibid., 224–25.

spiritual by this passage—that Paul was trying to teach about the "mysteries" of how human conduct would be evaluated by God. This is because, for Origen, civil authority was often self-evidently corrupt, violent, and unrighteous. It could not be that Paul meant us to obey and respect civil authorities without question, because Origen had lived through persecutions and had seen that civil authorities were not always worthy of respect. This is a theme that would be picked up by Christians for centuries: Romans 13 could not be as simple as it looks, because Christian experience told them that civil authorities were often *not* conduits of divine goodness. And, the farther the interpreter was from the centers of power, the more likely they were to conclude this. It's not surprising then that some of the most sustained wrestling with this chapter comes from Christians who lived under foreign colonizing powers. We will turn to some of those writers now.

Postcolonial Readings of Romans 13

Colonialism describes the situation in which one political entity occupies, exploits, and dominates another one. Often this is done through military force, and often colonialism results in the destruction or significant alteration of the colonized entity's culture, economy, traditions, religions, and people. The most prominent examples of colonialism have come from European nations colonizing places in Africa, Asia, and the Americas, especially from the fifteenth through the twenty-first centuries. Many of those European nations spread Christianity with them wherever they went, imposing their religion on the people they colonized. However, those colonized people have, in turn, used the interpretation of the Bible as a tool to combat their oppression, pointing to ways the colonizers misunderstood or misused their own religious traditions.

Emanuel Gerrit Singgih points out that in Indonesia, the interpretation of Romans 13 to defend civil authorities is known as the "colonial interpretation."[8] This is already very telling, as it maps out a history of colonizers (in his case, Dutch) invoking the passage to ensure that their rule was viewed as "correct." Colonial powers would naturally see their rule as unimpeachable, and they appealed to Paul's words to bolster their claim.

Also writing from a postcolonial perspective, Tarcisius Mukuka points out that Paul himself was a colonial subject, neither fully Roman nor fully Jewish, but embodying both identities while sliding between

[8]Emanuel Gerrit Singgih, "Towards a Postcolonial Interpretation of Romans 13:1–7: Karl Barth, Robert Jewett, and the Context of Reformation in Present-Day Indonesia," *Asia Journal of Theology* 23, no. 1 (April 2009): 111.

them.[9] His audience in Rome, too, could be thought of as hybrid, neither solidly on the side of the Roman Empire nor actively opposing it. Paul's letter, Mukuka points out, *has* to be read as Paul's attempt to thread that needle, and not as a confident statement of support for the power structures of empire. Paul lived in the Jewish diaspora, the dispersion of Jews across the Roman Empire, and he knew that any Jews his letter might find among his audience in Rome would similarly be diasporic. Paul's life ended before the most decisive event in the relationship between Rome and the Jews, the first Jewish War that culminated in the destruction of Jerusalem and much of the surrounding countryside in the year 70. Following that, the diaspora grew significantly, owing to Judeans fleeing the violence to places around the Empire to escape, and to Judean captives being sold into slavery across the Mediterranean. However, already in Paul's lifetime there were strong tensions between Jews and their Roman occupiers, as the events of the gospels illustrate. Mukuka is making a point that is very similar to the one I made at the beginning of this chapter: Paul had a lot more in common with those on the underside of Roman power than he did with those on top.

This had implications for some of things Paul talks about in Romans 13. Taxes, for a colonized subject, were a problem. "To pay taxes to a colonial power still occupying the homeland must have a potentially divisive issue" to Paul and any Jews in his audience, Mukuka says.[10] But, Paul's insistence that they be paid was likely in service to the gospel's harmonious spread in Rome. Paul must have thought it better to get along with the colonizers on this matter, Mukuka says. However, Mukuka's most significant observation comes in his qualification of what "authority" might mean. Here he uses a different but valid translation of the word that the NRSV translates "ruling," instead using "excelling." "In light of our understanding of authority above as one who 'promotes the increase and prosperity' of others," Mukuka writes, "the point of the exercise is to ask whether the prevailing authority is trying to excel in its authority and [is] therefore worthy of our submission."[11]

This kind of postcolonial reading understands authority very differently than readings that come from dominating cultures and societies. It recognizes that Paul, as a colonized subject himself, could not have meant what so many interpreters from European colonizing powers have supposed he meant. As a person who had been persecuted

---

[9]Tarcisius Mukuka, "Reading/Hearing Romans 13:1–7 under an African Tree: Towards a Lectio Postcolonica Contexta Africana," *New Testament Society of Southern Africa* 46, no. 1 (2012): 110–11.

[10]Ibid., 129.

[11]Ibid., 131.

by Roman power and who was a follower of Jesus, who had been crucified by Roman power, Paul would not have blithely advocated submitting to it.

Neil Elliott, one of the leading interpreters of Paul in light of empire, likewise sees Paul's comments in Romans 13:1–7 as "part of an ad-hoc survival strategy in an impossible situation."[12] Elliott sees Paul's language about being subject to the ruling authorities as the only possibility available to someone such as Paul, who saw the strength of the Roman state wielded against himself and his people and correctly calculated that subordinating himself to it was the only reasonable strategy. However, Elliott notes that compared to other endorsements of Roman power, especially the writings of Josephus a generation later, Paul's words sound limited and tepid. The mistake of modern interpreters is that they do not hear Paul's words in the context of others similar to him; Paul was like the man mumbling an allegiance pledge at a rally, not shouting it. In another of his works, Elliott says that in Romans 13 "we are in touch here with the constraining force of ideology, with the 'voice under domination.'"[13] Paul was saying the least that he could say, given his circumstances. We are still a long way from Jeff Sessions' confident claims that Romans 13 provides legitimacy for any government action.

The American Revolution and Romans 13

The colonial protest most familiar to many readers is the American Revolution. That war was fought by British colonies in North America against the British Empire. There were some key differences between this instance of colonialism and others; for instance, the war was largely fought by persons of English descent against the English government, and not by native people against invading outsiders. Still, many of the opinions in the Revolutionary War regarding Romans 13 mirror those in other colonial contexts. Historian James Byrd notes that the text was the subject of sermons by defenders of British power and revolutionaries alike.[14] A preacher named Jonathan Mayhew delivered a sermon in the lead-up to the Revolutionary War titled *Discourse Concerning Unlimited Submission and Non-Resistance to the Higher Powers,* while Charles Inglis preached a dueling sermon, *The Duty of Honoring the King.* From their titles, it's not hard to guess where these two preachers came down.

---

[12]Neil Elliott, "Romans," in *A Postcolonial Commentary on the New Testament Writings,* ed. Fernando F. Segovia and R.S. Sugirtharajah (London: T & T Clark, 2009), 211.

[13]Neil Elliott, *The Arrogance of Nations: Reading Romans in the Shadow of Empire,* Paul in Critical Contexts (Minneapolis: Fortress Press, 2008), 156.

[14]James P. Byrd, *Sacred Scripture, Sacred War: The Bible and the American Revolution* (New York: Oxford University Press, 2013), 123–24.

Inglis' sermon was actually based on 1 Peter 2:17, and not Romans 13, but the intent was the same: to show that God sanctioned the king, making him worthy of respect and obedience. Mayhew, meanwhile, followed an argument that will be familiar by now. Citing Paul's own complicated life as an imperial subject, Mayhew (according to Byrd) argued that Paul was calling for "obedience to just rulers and protest against unjust ones."[15]

Mayhew's sermon was remembered decades later, and was an inspiration for the Revolution, because he hadn't pulled any punches. His language was incendiary and forthright, especially when it came to criticizing rulers who were unjust—those who performed their duties poorly and exploited their constituents:

> When once magistrates act contrary to their office, and the end of their institution; when they rob and ruin the public, instead of being guardians of its peace and welfare; they immediately cease to be the *ordinance* and *ministers of God*; and no more deserve that glorious character than common *pirates* and *highwaymen*.[16]

Mayhew, as did Origen and other colonial subjects before him, felt that all power was not equally ordained by God, but that only power that operated justly could claim divine sanction. Reading Romans 13, Mayhew noted that the word "instituted" in the NRSV and "ordained" in the KJV implied that only those civil authorities worthy of ordination by God should be considered worthy of submission. For him, this excluded the British monarch.[17] Why submit to a government that itself did not submit to the will of God? Why pay taxes to a government that was set on fleecing its people through taxation? The seeds of revolution were present all through Mayhew's sermon. But once that revolution had been completed, the nation born of it faced a new crisis of government a few generations later, and Paul's words in Romans 13 were once again brought to the forefront.

The Fugitive Slave Act and Romans 13

In the previous chapter we saw how the Fugitive Slave Act of 1850 sparked debate over several parts of Paul's writings, most notably the

---

[15]James P. Byrd, *Sacred Scripture, Sacred War* (New York: Oxford, 2013), 124.

[16]Jonathan Mayhew, "A Discourse Concerning Unlimited Submission and Non-Resistance to the Higher Powers: With Some Reflections on the Resistance Made to King Charles I. And on the Anniversary of His Death: In Which the Mysterious Doctrine of That Prince's Saintship," (1750), ed. Paul Royster, *DigitalCommons@ University of Nebraska - Lincoln*, 24. https://digitalcommons.unl.edu/cgi/viewcontent.cgi?referer=https://www.google.com/&httpsredir=1&article=1044&context=etas

[17]Ibid., 26.

letter to Philemon. We saw how, in the *Weekly North Carolina Standard* newspaper, Paul was produced as an argument against Northern abolitionists who had pledged to aid and comfort runaway slaves. For the Southern newspaper, those actions were not only treasonous, but sacrilegious too, since in Romans 13 Paul had demanded submission to authorities. However, for the Northern Congregationalists (and other groups of abolitionists, both religious and nonreligious), Paul's words were not a call to obey just *any* civil authority or *any* statute without exception. Such groups understood themselves to have obligations to a higher truth.

I don't want to reproduce all of that material here, but I do want to point out that, in this debate, we finally see something that we haven't seen explicitly so far—not in Paul's own words, not in Origen's interpretation, and not in the postcolonial perspectives. Here, in the voices of the Northern abolitionists, we hear the first hints of a theology of civil disobedience. Historically, they were not, by any means, the first to advocate this position, and they would not be the last or the most important. But, in those Congregationalists and others similar to them, we begin to sense the outline of a theology that would become extremely important in American history, especially in the Civil Rights Era. The idea of refusing to acquiesce to a bad law or an illegitimate authority was one thing, but it was quite another to protest that law or authority actively. Furthermore, in each of the cases we have looked at so far, the question was whether subjects of a civil authority would submit, or not, but here we see an added dimension to the debate. With the Fugitive Slave Act, we see the question of whether a third party ought to protest and disobey civil authority for the purpose of *aiding someone else*. In a line—from the abolitionist movement to the act of kneeling during the National Anthem, and stretching through the women's suffrage movement and civil rights movement and the Vietnam War protests—a distinct strand of American political theology has demanded disobedience not only for one's own sake, but also for the sake of the neighbor. To return to the question of immigration, the question for Progressive Christians isn't really whether they should obey or disobey civil authorities in the way Jeff Sessions was asking. The question is whether they are willing to engage in civil disobedience, putting their own safety and prosperity on the line to defend those who are harmed by civil authorities employing their power unjustly.

A New Perspective Reading of Romans 13

One of the real benefits of a paradigm shift in interpretation, such as the New Perspective, is that it can help us to see things in a text that we simply could not have seen otherwise. For centuries, as we will see in the next chapter, Romans was thought of as a theological treatise— Paul's greatest essay on justification by faith and a roadmap to salvation. The New Perspective has helped us to see such theological reading of Romans as a much later layer of interpretation, not a part of the letter as Paul wrote it or as the communities in Rome would have received it. Instead, the New Perspective has helped us see a different kind of theme and unity to the letter, with the question of Jews and gentiles at the center. Beyond that, in recent years scholars have recognized that the letter served as a rationale for Paul's planned missionary journey to Spain.[18] Romans was a kind of ancient Kickstarter campaign—meant by Paul to introduce himself to the Jesus-following communities in Rome, yes, but especially to gain their financial and logistical support to help him get to Spain. Spain (on the far western edge of the Roman Empire), and the gentiles who lived there, was the obvious geographical conclusion of his career arc that spanned from Jerusalem westward.

When read through the New Perspective, Romans has a kind of unity that's very different from the unity provided by the Lutheran (or Traditional) Perspective. Instead of being about individual salvation and the self's plight through sin and redemption, Romans suddenly comes into focus as a sustained address to gentile Jesus-followers in the city. The letter starts to make sense as Paul's attempt to sort through the confusing situation in Rome, which is still mostly unknown to us today. Most of the letter deals with those questions, reaching a climax in chapters 9 through 11. Reading it this way, the suddenness of chapter 13 becomes less sudden. Where many interpreters have seen a jarring change in Paul's subject matter, the New Perspective helps us understand why Paul would begin talking about governing authorities when he had been talking about Jews and gentiles up to that point.

The argument hinges on one word. In English, it can be translated as two different words, but in the Greek, it's just one. In 13:3, the word translated as "rulers" in English versions is the Greek word *archontes*. *Archontes*, as with most words in most languages, has more than one meaning. There are two main meanings for this word. The first one, and the one most frequently used in English translations, is a civic leader ("ruler"), such as a prince or a king. That's the meaning that every interpreter we've investigated so far has presumed, and it's the meaning that Jeff Sessions had in mind when he evoked Paul's "wise command" to obey the "laws of the government" as a rationale for arresting immigrants and detaining children and parents separately.

---

[18]The most important work in this new understanding is Robert Jewett, *Romans: A Commentary* (Minneapolis: Fortress Press, 2007).

The other meaning, though, takes on new significance in light of the New Perspective. *Archontes* can also mean the leader or main authority in a non-civil sense. In the New Testament, it is very frequently used in the gospels to describe Jewish leaders—the Sanhedrin, synagogue officials, and the like. It's the word used for Nicodemus in John 3:1, the word used in the story of the "certain ruler" in Luke 18:18, the word used for the "leader of the Pharisees" in Luke 14:1, the word used for the "leader of the synagogue" (named Jairus in Luke) in Matthew 9:18 and Luke 8:41, and for other Jewish leaders in other places. Paul doesn't use the word very often, only two other times besides this instance in Romans—in both cases to talk about "rulers of this age" in 1 Corinthians 2:6 and 2:8, and it's hard to tell from that passage whether Paul means religious or civil authorities.

If we take *archontes* in Romans 13 to have its most common New Testament meaning of a *religious* leader, then a new range of interpretations opens up. Suddenly, Romans 13 looks less strange. Paul has just spent most of the letter talking to a mostly gentile audience about Jewish and gentile relations, and Romans 13 becomes a specific example of that. Paul might be giving his gentile readers the solution to a problem he knew they had: whether and how far to follow the authority of synagogue leaders.

Think about the possible situation in Rome. The Jewish community had been there before Jesus ever came along, and when Jesus-devotion spread to the city, some Jewish folks became believers in Jesus, and others did not. For Jewish Jesus-followers, it would have been natural to stay in the synagogues; after all, they were still wholly Jewish. Meanwhile, gentiles who became Jesus-followers might have found a natural home in the synagogues, too, but over time a tension began to form. What authority should a non-Jesus-following synagogue leader have over them? After all, these gentiles weren't Jews, exactly. Should they really have to do what the synagogue authorities said? In Romans 13, Paul might well have been telling them that yes, the authority of the synagogue leaders was divinely given, and they were ordained by God, and therefore you needed to respect them and submit to their authority.

But what about the taxes in verses 6 and 7? Reading this passage as dealing with synagogue leaders helps us understand that too. All Jews (priests excluded) were required to pay a tax for the upkeep of the temple; most of the time this was called the "temple tax." You can see this tax at work in Matthew 17:24–27, where Peter is confronted by "the collectors of the temple tax," asking whether Jesus pays the tax or not. It was an obligation of Jews to pay it, and a mark of inclusion in the community.

It's not hard to imagine that the Jesus-following, synagogue-going gentiles in Rome would have faced questions about this tax. Were these people Jews? This was a murky question in the early days of the church, but many Jesus-followers, Jews, and pagans thought that Jesus-following gentiles *were* a kind of Jew, and so needed to pay the tax. But, some gentiles would have grumbled about this. Why should they have to pay for the upkeep of a temple they had never visited, and at which they would never make a sacrifice? Here, Paul wraps the question of the tax with the question of respect. "Look," he is saying, "they were here before you, and you owe them your respect and submission because they were put in place by God. Pay the tax, because taxes are part and parcel of being a respectful, relatively new member of this community."

There's one final objection that might be raised by those who want to read Romans 13 to be about civil authority, and not synagogue authorities. In verse 4, Paul talks about "the sword" that authority wields. Since religious authorities generally do not carry or use swords, isn't this a signal that Paul must have been talking about civil authorities? Not at all. The Greek word that Paul used can definitely mean "sword" or "dagger," as in a literal weapon. But, it also has other meanings. It can mean "authority" in general (as it does in Ephesians 6:17), and it can refer to the general way authority is exercised. To "carry the sword" is something akin to our modern "wield the gavel" in a judicial sense. Judges don't literally carry a gavel everywhere they go, but it's a way of saying that they carry that authority with them. That's what Paul was talking about here in Romans 13:4: the authority that was given to religious leaders to discern truth from falsehood, right from wrong, and so forth.

Paul the Xenophobe?

I especially love this New Perspective reading of Romans 13, for two reasons. First, I love it because it solves some really thorny interpretive issues, such as why Paul switched gears so suddenly, and why a colonized subject such as Paul would advocate for submission to the colonizing power. It makes sense of a passage that hasn't really made all that much sense in the past, under other models of interpretation. But, I also love it because, if this interpretation is correct, then former United States Attorney General Jeff Sessions, by all accounts a conservative and devout United Methodist, is on record as suggesting that we all pay more attention to rabbis. I know that's definitely not what he meant, but he made a case for it by accident: every so often, it wouldn't hurt to be subject to synagogue leaders. From time to time, listen to the rabbis.

In a rare moment (though by accident), I think Jeff Sessions and I agree on something.

What we do not agree on is that Paul's words in Romans 13 could in any way excuse the United States immigration policy that Sessions helped craft and enforce. Throughout history, the only kinds of people who have interpreted Romans 13 the way Sessions is interpreting it have been those on the side of power, and trying to keep power for themselves. They were the Roman persecutors in Origen's day, the defenders of the British Empire in the 1700s onward, slaveholders in the 1850s, and colonial powers all over the globe. Sessions' interpretation of Paul's writings aligns him with those unsavory "colleagues," and others who have used scripture to excuse behavior that could never rise to the level of the "higher law" that we are called to follow. Paul would have stood on the side of immigrants, not the ICE agents tracking them down and arresting them. After all, as Paul proudly tells us in 2 Corinthians, he spent much of his life running from governments and slipping through their plans to catch and punish him. He lived his life on the underside of civil authority, trying to do what he thought was right *in spite of* the laws and rulers arrayed against him. He would have fit right in with the people Jeff Sessions was trying to intimidate, punish, and expel, but he wouldn't have had much in common with the government rulers of our age.

CHAPTER 8

Paul the Debt and Guilt Monger

If You Died Tonight

When I was a counselor at an evangelical summer camp, we went through lots of training. We were trained in first aid and CPR, in appropriate boundaries with campers and with other counselors, in how to play and facilitate games, in how to lead a dozen nine year olds on a campout—and we were trained in evangelism. There was always a part of orientation in which we learned how to talk to campers about their salvation: *If you died tonight, do you know where you would go? Have you ever made a decision for Christ? How certain are you? Have you ever prayed the sinner's prayer? Would you like to pray it now?* At the end of every week of camp, we would report back to the gathering of counselors and camp administrators about how many of our campers had "come to Christ" that week. Some counselors had impressive totals; they'd have three or four kids per week making professions of faith (though, really, most of the kids coming to the camp were *already* from very religious homes).

I was never very good at this part of the job. I held the "one-on-ones" with the campers in my cabins, sure. I actually really enjoyed those. But, in the same way I was terrible at my job selling furniture at a store in the mall during college, I was never any good at "closing the deal" with those campers. We usually just ended up talking for a while, out on the front porch of the cabin, while the rest of the campers hung out inside. One by one, those campers and I would shoot the breeze about their lives, talk about the week at camp, and talk about what they were going to do with the rest of their summer. As it came time to finish the conversation, I'd usually offer up some feeble attempt at evangelism—again, I was terrible at it—and they'd assure me that, yes, they were Christians who went to church, and I'd tell them how much fun it had been having them in the cabin that week, and I'd move on to the next kid.

One summer when I was a senior counselor, I got the cabin list for the next week. On the list was the name of a notorious camper—I'll call him Wilson. This kid had been to camp for a few years, and he was renowned as a difficult person to have in your cabin. Wilson had behavior issues, problems with authority, and trouble sitting still and being quiet for things such as Bible study. I groaned when I saw his name, and I sort of grimaced when I saw him walking up to the cabin on check-in day. However, it turned out that Wilson wasn't so bad. He could be "scattered," sure, but he also had an outgoing personality, a good sense of humor, and a knack for leadership. He was the kind of kid who was actually pretty great to have in your cabin because the other kids naturally rallied around him.

When it was time for Wilson and I to have our one-on-one, we went out to the front porch of the cabin to talk. I started with the usual small talk: what did he like to do back at home, what were his plans, what were his favorite parts of camp, and so on. However, before long, Wilson was crying. He told me about the trouble in his parents' marriage. He told me about how he struggled in school, and didn't really fit in. He started sharing all kinds of things about his life, and after a while I told him to sit tight, and I went and grabbed my personal stash of snacks. I handed him a bag of chips, and we sat out there on the porch and talked for a couple of hours—long past the usual ten or fifteen minutes. When it got late, I knew I was supposed to start asking Wilson those questions: *Do you know Jesus as your personal Lord and Savior? Would you like to invite him into your heart tonight?* But, I couldn't do it. I knew that would be the wrong thing to do. I was only eighteen or nineteen years old myself, but I realized that to ask Wilson those questions in that moment would have been a violation of trust.

I didn't ask Wilson those questions that night, and I never asked any campers those questions again. I had reached an understanding with myself—which Wilson had helped me comprehend—that personal salvation was not what most kids needed from their camp counselor. They needed someone who genuinely cared about them as persons, who listened, and who treated them kindly. As for me, I knew that evangelism was no longer part of my role. I didn't begrudge my fellow counselors their gaudy statistics at the end of every week, but I had drawn a line that I wouldn't cross again. I was still an *evangelical* in many ways, and would be for a few more years, but I was no longer an *evangelist*. In hindsight, that was also around the time the evangelical view of salvation began to unravel for me. Partly because of prodding by my pastor and my college classes, and partly because of experiences such as the one with Wilson, I stopped being certain that asking Jesus into one's heart was the primary goal and event of salvation. I began to think about Jesus in different ways.

That script that we were taught during counselor training relied heavily on Paul. In fact, in most versions, it all came from the book of Romans. Often, the whole thing is called the "Romans Road" to salvation. It all made perfect sense when they put it up on the projector during one-on-one training. There was a series of steps you were supposed to walk the person through, beginning with the problem of the human condition and ending with the answer that could be found in Jesus. The steps usually looked something along these lines:

- Recognize that God is the sovereign creator of the universe and of me individually, and recognize that we are subordinate to God (Rom. 1:20–21)

- Realize that "all have sinned and fall short of the glory of God," and that includes me (Rom. 3:23)

- Understand that Jesus has paid the penalty for our sins, including mine (Rom. 5:8)

- Know that without Jesus, we are doomed to perish because of our sin, including me (Rom. 6:23)

- Confess the name of Jesus as our Lord and Savior, having faith in Jesus as the only one who can deliver us from our sin (Rom. 10:9–10)

- Be assured that this simple act—and no other action or work by us—is sufficient for salvation (Rom. 10:13)

- Make Jesus the Lord of our life (Rom. 11:36)

That was it. The "sinner's prayer" usually came somewhere around "step 5," the confession, during which we were supposed to invite the person to pray for Jesus to become their savior. That was the key part; even if that's all that happened, the doctrine of "assurance of salvation" meant that our campers—or whoever else we "witnessed to"—were saved.

There's a topic of conversation that comes up every so often with my ex-evangelical friends: How many times did you "get saved?" Despite the presence of "assurance of salvation" on that list, almost nobody got saved only once. Some got saved every summer at their church camp. Others got saved every time they started attending a new youth group. Personally, I think my number is three, starting with an awkward conversation at a vacation Bible school meeting when I was about eight years old. People got saved over and over, because the system was fueled by fear of damnation, and it was better to be safe than sorry, wasn't it? If Paul was right in Romans 3:23—if "all have sinned and fall short of the glory of God"—then the doubt would always catch up to you, making you wonder whether you *really* had faith, whether you *really* were on the list, whether you *really* would go to heaven if you died that night.

A couple of decades later, as a Bible scholar and a historian of religion, I understand a lot more about those experiences of my youth. That camp where I was a counselor was deeply rooted in a tradition that came out of the Protestant Reformation, and it was strongly pushing a Reformation model of salvation. In this model, only faith—defined as *belief*—and not anything else, could save you. The book of Romans was the most important handbook of salvation that we possessed. We all owed a debt to God, because of our wicked sinful nature, and we were unable to pay that debt, no matter how many good deeds we did or how many church services we attended. Only faith in Jesus was sufficient to pluck us up out of the hellfire we otherwise deserved. It was all laid out clearly by Paul, the great explainer of salvation, who had written it out clearly in what we all called the "Romans Road" to salvation.

The Road to the Romans Road to Salvation

By this point in the book, you know what to expect from me. I've just described the way many Christians have thought about Paul for a long time, and now I'm going to reemphasize how wrong we've all been about him—how Paul is really very different than the person we thought him to be. And yes, that is what I am going to do. But more than any of the other misunderstandings in this book—more than Paul the misogynist, more than Paul the homophobe, more than Paul the anti-Semite, more than Paul the prude, more than Paul the slavery apologist, more than Paul the xenophobe—when we misunderstand Paul as the architect of this guilt-, and shame-, and debt-based system of salvation, we get Paul spectacularly, wretchedly, totally wrong.

Once again, the road to this bad interpretation of Paul runs right through the life of Martin Luther. Luther is the best-known figure of the Protestant Reformation, and, along with John Calvin, he was the originator of some of the most important theological claims to emerge from that period.

A brief recap: Martin Luther was an Augustinian monk in Germany, and he was possessed by feelings of sinful inadequacy.[1] Luther felt

[1]Glenn S. Sunshine, *A Brief Introduction to the Reformation* (Louisville: Westminster John Knox Press, 2017), 13–24.

like he was a helpless sinner before God, completely unable to atone for his sins or even control them. His days were consumed with this problem; Luther dwelled on the question of how he could possibly make things right with a perfect and sinless God, when he himself was so completely mired in his depraved humanity. At the same time, Luther was becoming concerned by some of the church practices in his part of Germany. The church was trying to raise money to pay for the new St. Peter's Basilica in Rome, and one of the methods by which they were doing this was the sale of *indulgences*. An indulgence was a certificate from the church waiving the punishment for sin, and it could be received in exchange for a financial contribution. Protestants have been trained to feel outraged at this practice, but really it was only a slight innovation over longstanding church practices; for centuries, the church had allowed people to undertake tasks (or good works) to help counterbalance their sin. A person could, for example, go on a pilgrimage, give alms to the poor, or help fund the renovation of a monastery. An indulgence, like those things, involved an expenditure of money, but the money wasn't really the main point. An indulgence, as with many ways of doing penance, was a way of expressing remorse and atoning for misdeeds.

Itinerant indulgence preachers were often the ones who promoted these indulgences, and, unfortunately, the indulgence preacher sent to Luther's neighborhood was one of the most craven and opportunistic of them all. Johann Tetzel had more in common with a pawn shop owner or a bail bondsman than he did a priest; legend has it that he went around selling indulgences with slogans along the lines of, "As soon as the coin in the coffer rings, the soul to heaven springs." This, to Luther (and many others) was naked, cynical predatory penance. Peasants who couldn't afford food were purchasing indulgences for their dead relatives, hoping to ease their time in purgatory, or they were spending their last coin on an indulgence in hopes that it would free them from damnation. Luther was aghast.

These two things—disgust at the sale of indulgences, and the feeling of worthless helplessness before God—coalesced in Luther. He began to protest publicly against indulgences (this is what the "95 Theses" were about) and he also began to rethink the way salvation worked in the church. To make a long story short, Martin Luther reread the New Testament, especially Paul, and most particularly Romans, in light of his predicament. He saw Paul's words in Romans as a correction to the use of good works to expiate sins, and he recognized in Paul someone who had dealt with the same kind of struggle—the struggle to be reconciled with God.

"I do not understand my own actions," Paul wrote in Romans 7. "For I do not do what I want, but I do the very thing that I hate... But in fact it is no longer I that do it, but sin that dwells within me" (vv. 15, 17). Many modern scholars think that Paul was speaking in someone else's voice here, in something called "diatribe style," in the way we might say something today and use "air quotes" with our hands to indicate that the ideas belong to someone else. But Luther saw himself in these words and other words of Paul's, and he recognized his own struggle in Paul's struggle. And all of this helped give him a framework for critiquing the church's focus on good works (such as buying indulgences) as a part of attaining salvation.

Luther was well-primed to have just this epiphany. He was, after all, a monk in the order named after Augustine of Hippo, the great intellectual of the ancient church. Augustine, too, wrestled with his own sinful nature, although Augustine seems to have clung affectionately to his sins longer than Luther did, since he famously prayed as a youth, "Lord give me chastity and continence, but not yet."[2] In Augustine, Luther found a companion in his self-doubt and self-contemplative journeys, and Luther read Augustine, who was in turn reading Paul, creating a very powerful textual community for him. The more Luther read Paul, and read Augustine reading Paul, the more Luther began to experience Christianity in new ways.

We've already seen how much Luther adored and relied on Paul, and especially Romans. He called it "the most important piece in the New Testament," and "purest Gospel."[3] In Romans, Luther discerned a new way of understanding salvation. Instead of performing good works, such as buying indulgences and saying prayers, Luther began to frame salvation in terms of *justification by faith*. "Justification," or *dikaiosyne* in the Greek, means something along the lines of "righteousness" or "uprightness." Paul used this word four times in Romans and twice in his other letters to describe a state of humanity being right with God.[4] For example, in Romans 4:25 Paul writes that Jesus "was handed over to death for our trespasses and was raised for our justification," and in Romans 5:18 he writes that "one man's act of righteousness leads to justification and life for all." Paul clearly understood Jesus to be the key to human beings' reconciliation and rightness with God. Luther picked up on that language, and he developed a theology that focused strongly on that role of Jesus. By grace alone are our sins forgiven, the

---

[2]Confessions 7.7.17.

[3]Martin Luther, "Preface to the Letter of St. Paul to the Romans," trans. Bro. Andrew Thornton, OSB, n.d., chap. 1.1, accessed at https://www.ccel.org/l/luther/romans/pref_romans.html.

[4]Romans 4:25; 5:16; 5:18; 5:21; 2 Corinthians 3:9; Galatians 2:21.

Reformation doctrine went, and by faith alone is that grace attained. That meant that for Luther and others like him, the justification that Paul talked about in Romans was available only through Jesus and only by faith in Jesus, and not by any good work or deed that a human being could do. Buying an indulgence wouldn't get you anywhere; you needed to have faith in Jesus' power to save you from your sin—and, if you had faith, Jesus would save you.

You can see how that Reformation-era thinking developed into the "Romans Road" training I received as a camp counselor. This way of thinking about salvation has become the default for most Protestant denominations today—and, even for many non-Christians, some version of "Jesus died for your sins and you just have to believe in him" is the thumbnail sketch in their minds of how they think Christians believe Christianity works. It's a powerful and durable way of framing salvation, because it is so simple. Believe in Jesus, and Jesus takes care of the rest. Even baptism, we were told in camp counselor evangelism training, is "the first act of obedience." It's nice to do, but it's not necessary. Salvation happens when you invite Jesus into your *heart,* not through any ritual.

However, if this has become the default understanding of how salvation works, for many progressive Christians and non-Christians it has also become the default understanding of the religion they *don't* believe in. When I've talked with former evangelicals and former Christians about their reasons for leaving conservative churches or leaving church altogether, this debt-based system of salvation often comes up. Remember, this system got its start with Martin Luther's feelings of sinful inadequacy. Its starting point for human nature is that we are all awful, fallen, sinful creatures—"totally depraved," to use a common phrase from John Calvin's work. A commonly cited passage from Romans, which is itself quoting parts of the Hebrew Bible, gets the point across:

> "There is no one who is righteous, not even one;
>> there is no one who has understanding,
>>> there is no one who seeks God.

> All have turned aside, together they have become worthless;
>> there is no one who shows kindness,
>>> there is not even one."

> "Their throats are opened graves;
>> they use their tongues to deceive."
> "The venom of vipers is under their lips."
>> "Their mouths are full of cursing and bitterness."

"Their feet are swift to shed blood;
    ruin and misery are in their paths,
and the way of peace they have not known."
    "There is no fear of God before their eyes."
    (Rom. 3:10–18)

This is a pretty bleak view of human nature, and for many people the constant reminders that they are fallen, wretched, sinful creatures become an unbearable burden. In this theology there is no trace of the "it was good" that God spoke at creation in Genesis. There is only the fallenness of the world and the baseness of humans. The point of this emphasis on fallenness is to convince and remind people that they are utterly helpless before God, and completely in need of a savior. But, for many people it has the effect of making religion completely about the guilt and shame of being who you are, and the need for someone else to pay the unpayable debt that you have accrued simply by existing.

Because it relies so heavily on Romans, Paul is usually the person who gets the blame for this debt- and guilt-based system of salvation. People assume that it was Paul who took the religion *of* Jesus and turned it into a religion *about* Jesus. Paul is the one, they say, who turned a beautiful tradition into an ever-turning hamster wheel of unpayable debts owed to God and unquenchable shame of being human. However, in reality this system doesn't have very much to do with Paul at all. He might not even recognize it. This message of debt, shame, and guilt is a long way from what Paul preached.

Rethinking Salvation in Paul

One of the great gifts of the New Perspective on Paul is that it helps us escape from the patterns of reading Paul in which we've been stuck since Martin Luther and the 1500s. We can trade out our old lenses for new ones, and suddenly we can see new things in the text that were obscured for centuries. The New Perspective has been especially good at helping scholars see that Paul was not anti-Semitic or anti-Jewish, as pointed out in chapter 4 of this book. However, because the New Perspective (and especially the Radical New Perspective) has not really made its way into many congregations yet, not as much attention has been paid to the way it can help us to rethink salvation.

What is challenging about salvation in Paul's writings is that he never really stops to say what he thinks salvation is, or how it works. This shouldn't surprise us, because Paul's letters were *letters,* and not theological tracts. If he had preached about salvation when he was in Corinth, there would be no reason for him to repeat himself in his letters to the Corinthians. Paul never lays out a system of salvation, perhaps because he assumes that his readers already know it from his preaching. Another possibility is that Paul and other first-century followers of Jesus just didn't think in terms of salvation in the way that we do today. The idea that salvation should be a central concern of religion is a modern one. Salvation wasn't a very big concern in the Judaism of Paul's time, for instance. There was certainly a sense that God was on the side of Israel and would defend and embrace Israel, but that didn't necessarily follow into an idea of individual salvation as modern Christianity thinks about it. Salvation in ancient Israel was national, this-worldly, and communal. So, maybe Paul simply wasn't thinking in the same terms in which we think.

I like the way Pamela Eisenbaum frames this problem. "Paul's letter to the Romans is not an answer to the question, How can I be saved? Rather," she writes, "it is his answer to the question, How will the world be redeemed, and how do I faithfully participate in that redemption?"[5] This is a huge and important distinction, and it's one that has the potential to help progressive Christians come to see Paul as an ally. For Paul, an individual asking about personal salvation didn't make much sense. The individual wasn't the problem. The problem was that the world was about to draw to a conclusion, and while Israel had long been reconciled to God and bound to God in covenant, gentiles were on the outside looking in. The gentiles had not been *justified*, to use Paul's language. The crisis Paul faced was that, as a class of human beings, gentiles had not been made "right" with God.

Jesus was the answer to this crisis, but, for Paul, Jesus was the *communal* answer, not the *individual* answer. This can be a hard shift for modern Christians to make, because we've been conditioned to think in terms of our individual status with God. As a Jewish person, Paul thought communally. It was Israel that God saved, not Israelites. Likewise, Paul understood that Jesus was the decisive event in God's plan to save gentiles—not as individuals, but as a collection of people. In the same way that God had intervened in history to form a relationship with Jews, in the form of covenant, God was now intervening in history to form a relationship with gentiles, and that intervention came in the form of Jesus. Jesus' life, death, and resurrection signaled a new initiative by God, in the last days, to bring gentiles into God's family.

There's one section of Romans that deserves special mention. In Romans 11, Paul produces one of his best-known allegories: the olive tree. This is Paul's attempt to describe the relationship between Israel and the gentiles, although exactly what Paul meant to convey is the subject of debate. (Krister Stendahl notes that Paul was a city kid, and

[5]Pamela Eisenbaum, *Paul Was Not a Christian: The Original Message of a Misunderstood Apostle* (New York: HarperOne, 2009), 252.

didn't seem to understand grafting).[6] There seem to be both communal and individual components of this allegory: the tree is the whole, while branches of the tree might represent individual persons or categories of people. Paul seems to intend this allegory mostly as a warning to his gentile audience, for them to guard against arrogance and haughtiness with respect to Jews. Ironically, most Christian interpreters have read it the other way around: as Paul triumphantly describing the way gentiles have displaced Jews in the tree. In his notes on this passage, Mark Nanos points out that the Greek is ambiguous, while the NRSV is unequivocal. Verse 17 and the first clause of 18 in the NRSV reads: "But if some of the branches were broken off, and you, a wild olive shoot, were grafted in their place to share the rich root of the olive tree, do not boast over the branches." A more literal translation would be: "But if some of the branches were bent, and you, a wild olive shoot, were grafted in among them to share the rich root of the olive tree, do not boast over the branches."[7] This is quite a difference, and Nanos' version fits much better with the point that Paul seems to be trying to get across: not that Israel has been cut off, but that gentiles have been let in. Bent, broken, or grafted, the effect of the allegory is that God is multiplying the sustenance provided by the one root.

How did this work? How were gentiles brought into right relationship with God? Well, here again we have to abandon categories that traditional Protestant Christianity has taught us. There's a mismatch between our modern categories and the ancient ones that Paul used and thought with. We might be tempted to answer that gentiles simply needed to believe in Jesus in order to come into right relationship with God, but it wasn't as simple as that. Belief didn't play the same role in ancient religion that it plays for many modern ones. People could believe in the existence of gods without worshiping those gods; belief was a separate category from devotion or belonging. A person of his time, Paul didn't seem to place very much emphasis on belief. As we have already seen, in his letters Paul wrote much more about ethics and community than he did about truth-claims. He wrote a great deal about righteousness, but not much about mental or spiritual agreement to propositions. And, Paul very often wrote about faith.

Here too we are limited by our prior knowledge of a term. For us, "faith" can mean something very similar to "belief." To "have faith" can mean something along the lines of "to believe something is true," even without evidence. But, that's not what Paul meant by it at all. The word

---

[6]Krister Stendahl, *Final Account: Paul's Letter to the Romans* (Minneapolis: Fortress, 1995), 37.

[7]Mark Nanos, "Notes on Romans," in *The Jewish Annotated New Testament,* 2d ed. (Oxford: Oxford University Press, 2017), 310.

in Greek is *pistis,* and it has been one of the most argued-about words in the debate over the New Perspective. *Pistis* can mean faith, in the sense we understand it today, as an intellectual commitment. But, it can also mean something such as trust, faithfulness, reliability, commitment, confidence, or trustworthiness. *Pistis* as Paul used it had a much wider range of nuance and meaning than the way we usually use the word *faith* today. And, this range of meanings is complicated further by an ambiguous grammatical construction that Paul sometimes used: *pistis christou.*

If you look in your Bible at Galatians 2:16, Romans 3:22, and Philippians 3:9, you'll see this phrase translated as "faith in Christ" or "faith in Jesus Christ." This fits very well with the Lutheran Perspective, which understands having faith in Jesus' saving power as fundamental to salvation. But, part of the reason that it fits so well is that Luther himself influenced this translation. Aside from being an eminent theologian and church reformer, Luther was also an extremely important translator of the Bible. While in hiding from his enemies during the 1520s, Luther set out to translate the Bible into German, at that time one of the most dangerous and transgressive things you could do (because the assumption was that the Bible should remain in Latin, not be translated into the "vulgar" tongues). When he came to these passages, Luther turned the ambiguous Greek into much less ambiguous German. That removal of ambiguity has carried through to almost all English translations since.

In Greek, *pistis christou* is a genitive construction. Genitives can do several different things, and, in this case, there are two possibilities. I'll spare you the specifics of the grammar; the two options are to translate this as "faith in Christ" or "the faithfulness of Christ."[8] The first option, *faith in Christ,* made perfect sense to Luther, and so he translated it that way, removing the ambiguity of the Greek when he rendered it into German. If Jesus was the one who could justify us with God, Luther thought, and belief in that fact is what saved us, then having faith in Christ was obviously the kind of thing Paul would say. In Luther's translation, putting faith in Jesus was the critical act of religion—the thing that eliminated our depravity and made us acceptable before God.

However, the other way of translating it, *the faithfulness of Christ,* is equally correct grammatically, perhaps even more so.[9] In this way of

---

[8]For a much more detailed explanation, see Eisenbaum, *Paul Was Not a Christian,* 191–94.

[9]Scholars argue ferociously about this. For a dense but comprehensive overview, see Richard B. Hays, *The Faith of Jesus of Christ* (Grand Rapids, Mich.: Wm. B. Eerdmans, 1983).

translating it, what matters is *not* the individual's agreement to the fact that Jesus is the divine mediator. What matters is that Jesus himself was faithful to the calling of God—that Jesus was, and is, trustworthy in the role he had to play. The different meanings of *pistis* can help flesh this out: we can have confidence in Christ, we can rely on Christ, and we can trust Christ *because* Jesus himself has been faithful in what God sent him to do. The faith (or faithfulness) belongs to Jesus, not to us. Humans' belief or unbelief in the saving power of Jesus isn't what saves them. Instead, what saves us is Jesus' obedience to his mission.

This can be a difficult conceptual shift to make, but once you make it, a lot of things click into place. It helps to make sense of some of Paul's behavior, for one thing. I've always wondered about Paul's comments in Romans 15:18–29, near the end of his letter, in which he gives the Romans a status report on his mission. "[F]rom Jerusalem and as far around as Illyricum," Paul writes in 15:19, "I have fully proclaimed the good news of Christ." The Greek there doesn't actually say "fully proclaimed"; it says "completed" or "fulfilled" the good news. Paul thinks he's "done" in the east, all the way from Jerusalem to what's now the neighborhood of Croatia. He goes on to say that, having finished his work in the east, he wants to head west toward Rome and ultimately to Spain, which makes sense when you plot his missionary work on a map. The main places west of where Paul had already "completed" his work were Italy and Spain.

However, Paul's claim to have "completed" or "fulfilled" his work in the eastern empire, or even to have "fully proclaimed" the good news, as the NRSV puts it, doesn't make any sense if we think about salvation in the modern Protestant sense. There were millions of people in the eastern Empire, and Paul had not evangelized them all. He had set up perhaps a dozen churches, scattered throughout Greece and Asia Minor, each community numbering maybe in the dozens of members. He barely made it out of the major cities; most people in the countryside probably had never heard of Paul or Jesus. In no modern sense had Paul "completed" his work, if the work of a missionary of the gospel is "witnessing" in the sense that many modern Christians understand it. He could not have evangelized every person.

That's because Paul was doing "wholesale" evangelism, not "retail." He didn't need to talk to every gentile, because individual gentiles' responses didn't matter. What mattered was, as Eisenbaum puts it, the answer to that question of, "How will the world be redeemed, and how do I faithfully participate in that redemption?"[10] Paul thought that Jesus was the mechanism by which God was redeeming the world's

---

[10]Eisenbaum, *Paul Was Not a Christian*, 252.

unrighteous—gentiles—and that his job was to gather communities of gentiles to bear witness to that fact. Just as not every Jew needed to keep the law perfectly for Israel to be God's people, not every gentile needed to respond to the invitation in order for gentiles to be justified. Paul needed outposts among the gentiles, representative samples so that God would see the faithful response. And, once Paul had established those outposts in the east, there was no need to wait for every single gentile to sign up. He was ready to move to the west.

What Is Jesus For?

So far, I've been talking about Jesus' role in vague terms: Jesus is the means by which God has offered justification to gentiles. But, how exactly does this work? How does Jesus "save"? This was a question with a number of different answers in ancient Christianity, and even within the New Testament. The book of Hebrews has a different answer than the Gospel of Luke, which is different from John, because they were all written in a time before Christianity had settled on any stable answers. For Paul, two things were important about Jesus: First was his faithfulness. It was important that Jesus, like Moses and Abraham before him, was faithful to his calling: *pistis christou*. Second were Jesus' death and resurrection. Paul saw a sign in Jesus' obedience to crucifixion and his subsequent resurrection. Jesus' resurrection was a sign that God had begun overturning death itself, breaking the power that death had on the world. In 1 Corinthians 15:20–23, as part of a larger section about death and resurrection, Paul writes:

> But in fact Christ has been raised from the dead, the first fruits of those who have died. For since death came through a human being, the resurrection of the dead has also come through a human being; for as all die in Adam, so will all be made alive in Christ. But each in his own order: Christ the first fruits, then at his coming those who belong to Christ.

This is a window into Paul's thinking: Jesus is the first of the resurrection, but not the last. Jesus is a new Adam, the one who will restore what Adam broke, or defeat the death that Adam introduced into the human experience.

Perhaps you noticed something about that passage from 1 Corinthians: that Paul calls Jesus a "human being." This is hardly a problem in mainstream modern Christianity, where the "fully divine, fully human" solution from the Council of Nicaea still holds. But Paul lived *before* Nicaea, and when he calls Jesus a "human being" he doesn't have Nicene orthodoxy in mind. Paul calls Jesus a human because

Paul's language almost always makes God the actor or agent, not Jesus. For Paul, Jesus does not *rise*; Jesus is *raised by God*.[11] Paul always talks about Jesus's resurrection in the passive voice, as in "he was raised," or in the active voice with God as the actor or agent, as in "God raised Jesus." Likewise, Paul prays to God, not to Jesus. Eisenbaum, following James D.G. Dunn, notes that Paul speaks about "'gospel of God,' 'son of God,' 'beloved of God,' 'the will of God,' 'the glory of God,'" and so on, pointing always to God as the ultimate author of the story.[12] In Paul's language and theology, God is always the final agent of action and source of divine thought, and Jesus is the one who was sent by that God to fulfill a particular mission—which he did faithfully. But, notice that Paul never says much at all about Jesus' life, only about his death and resurrection. Aside from telling the story of the Last Supper in 1 Corinthians, Paul doesn't relate stories about Jesus' life. But he does frequently proclaim Jesus' death and resurrection, because, for Paul, those were the important things—Jesus' faithfulness even to death, and God raising Jesus back to life.

This is not to minimize or erase Jesus. For Paul, Jesus is the key to the whole thing. Jesus' death and, especially, his resurrection are what gave gentiles a life raft at the end of the world, because, remember—Paul was convinced that that end was right around the corner. Jesus was a trustworthy and faithful figure who did the extraordinarily difficult thing God asked of him, and became the means of justification—although Paul doesn't ever quite spell out exactly how. But it was always God doing the *doing,* in the end. Jesus, like Adam, Abraham, and Moses, was a human who played a decisive role, and who upon his resurrection assumed an eternal place with God.

Taking stock of all of this, I'm led to wonder whether Paul was a "universalist"—someone who believed that, in the end, God would reconcile with, or "save," *all* people, not just some. The label might not have made sense to Paul, since he didn't start from a perspective of individual salvation to begin with. But, when he talks about the role Jesus played, and when he talks about his own experience of God's call and his own expectations of the work God was doing among the gentiles, Paul seems to presume that God was in the process of reconciling or justifying *all* gentiles. Paul seems to think this is true regardless of individual gentiles' responses to or even knowledge of Jesus. Jesus was the first fruits of a general resurrection, reversing the power of death for all, and Jesus was also the one justifying sinful

---

[11]Both Eisenbaum and Stendahl point to many examples of the theocentric "God-language" of Paul: Eisenbaum, *Paul Was Not a Christian,* 180–81; Stendahl, *Final Account,* 38–39.

[12]Eisenbaum, *Paul Was Not a Christian,* 180; James D.G. Dunn, *The Theology of Paul the Apostle* (Grand Rapids, Mich.: Wm. B. Eerdmans, 1998), 40.

gentiles in the eyes of God. Paul's comments in Romans 15 lead me to think that he thought in universalist terms—that the gospel was "fully proclaimed" or "completed" in the east when he had established representative witness communities of gentile Jesus-followers, not when every single gentile had individually become a follower of Jesus. Paul certainly seems to have thought that Jesus' death and resurrection were decisive events that came near the end of time, not an intermediate step that would lead to years, decades, or centuries of evangelism until all gentiles were convinced. He seems to have thought that if he could reach a few, then all would be saved.

A Progressive Christian Reading of Paul

The New Perspective on Paul does a great job of helping us see just how artificial the Lutheran Perspective's view of Paul is, and just how much that traditional debt-, guilt-, and shame-based system of salvation depends on Luther's way of understanding Paul. However, since the New Perspective has been an academic pursuit, carried out mostly by biblical scholars, the implications for a constructive Christian theology are still not very well articulated. Krister Stendahl, one of the earliest and most important architects of what has become known as the New Perspective, was a Lutheran bishop and biblical scholar, and he fused these two worlds together beautifully.[13] Yet I still see very little New Perspective thought finding its way into churches, so I want to spend a few moments now outlining what I see as its implications for progressive Christian theology. I do so with the caveat that I am not a theologian by any measure. What follows will be unsatisfying as theology, but I hope to point in some directions that theologians can explore.

The first and most obvious implication has to do with human nature. The Lutheran Perspective has what is called a "low anthropology"—a low view of human nature. It has thought of human beings as fallen, sinful, depraved creatures in abject need of saving—and otherwise helpless. This negative view of human nature has had profound consequences for individuals and for communities. It has devalued the world we live in as a temporary waiting room for heaven, making any effort to change or improve social realities seem futile. If human beings are categorically bad, then there's no sense changing anything, since human nature won't change this side of heaven.

In my experience, progressive Christianity strives to see the good in human beings and the potential in this world. Progressive Christianity often has what is called a "high anthropology"—a high opinion of the

---

[13]My favorite book by Stendahl is the thin and affordable *Final Account* (which has been cited previously in this book).

potential of human beings and their capacity to do good and effect change. Progressive Christianity is often engaged on the front lines of social change: fighting racism, sexism, homophobia, environmental destruction, and the like. Progressive Christians are convinced of the potential of human beings, and, in this, Paul is their ally. That might sound like a strange claim when it's made about a man who believed that the world was ending any time, and who sometimes actively discouraged people from trying to change their circumstances. But, Paul was not a moral nihilist. Remember, he was always cajoling his gentile churches to do better—to live more fully like the body of Christ they were called to be. As a follower of the Jewish law, Paul understood the human capacity to rise to a moral standard, and he often called on his gentile communities to do the same.

That leads to the second implication of the New Perspective on Paul for progressive Christians, which is an emphasis on community. In the balance between individuals and community, Paul chose community every time. In this we can find some really helpful tools for *ecclesiology,* or "thinking about the church." Paul called on the people in his congregations to put aside selfishness and work together for the common good. He recognized a variety of gifts, each mutually reinforcing the others. Paul understood the church—not the individual— to be the essential expression of his work. In his letters, Paul was always trying to bridge divides between or among individuals, and he was always calling on those individuals to subvert their own needs or desires to those of the community. I have experienced tensions in every church or religious community of which I have ever been a part—tensions over both belief and practice—and sometimes it feels as if this is especially true for progressive congregations. In a community that is not tightly bound by dogma or strict adherence to a common creed, what holds things together? Paul, with his emphasis on the sanctity of community for its own sake and as an expression of Christ's presence in the world, offers an incredible paradigm.

The third implication follows closely, and also relates to ecclesiology: when viewed through the Radical New Perspective, a high value on *inclusion* is built in to Paul's writings and career. Every letter he wrote was in some way concerned with the problems of inclusion and exclusion, and the ways communities could navigate boundaries. The premise of his whole career was outreach to gentiles, who he felt were in danger of permanent exclusion. He alienated some of his fellow Jews through his insistence that God was including gentiles, and he angered some gentiles because of perceived threats to their status quo. But, Paul's emphasis was always on broadening the horizon, always on reaching those who had been excluded. We don't know whether he ever made it to Spain, but it certainly seems that he wanted to try, reaching for the ends of the earth in his attempt to include people. He worked with and supported women in his churches, as we have seen, and he showed consistent concern for those who were on the underside of society. Paul was a visionary for inclusion, always trying to expand the circle, in a way that should inform and inspire us. He understood that diversity was a virtue.

The fourth implication is a little less well defined, but over the years I have seen students respond so positively to it that I know it must have transformative potential. The New Perspective reading of Paul can help us reconfigure our view of justification—how God is working to be reconciled with every human being. This doesn't begin from a place of abject depravity, as traditional Protestant theology does, but from a place of God's initiative. The Hebrew Bible describes how God sought out a relationship with Israel, and in Paul's writings we see God seeking out a relationship with gentiles. God, as the creator and author of the universe, is justifying us together by the faithfulness of Jesus. Jesus is still central to our faith, but not because he is a god masquerading as a human. Jesus is central because he is the human sent from God, faithfully fulfilling his calling and calling all of us to do the same. Here, Paul's writings can point the way toward a rethinking of Christology that isn't predicated on the old spectrum of high-to-low (a span of divine-to-human Jesus), but that instead rests on Jesus as emblematic of God's saving work. The question of Jesus' divinity is less important to Paul than the fact that Jesus points to the lengths to which God will go in order to include. It's not about high Christology or low Christology, it's about Christ as the pattern of God's saving work in the world.

Finally, I return to the question Pamela Eisenbaum thought Paul was asking, the question about eschatology: How will the world be redeemed, and how do I participate faithfully in that redemption? Krister Stendahl asked a very similar question, but in a different way—and one that makes sense to me given my camp counseling experiences. "There are two ways of thinking about God," he said. "One way is to imagine a God who asks, first thing every morning, 'What are the statistics on the saved?' Another is to have a God who first asks, 'Has there been any progress for the kingdom?'"[14] Paul understood God in that second way, and Paul seems to have understood that he played a large role in that potential progress for the kingdom. Progressive Christians naturally ask that second question about progress for the kingdom, and we naturally

---

[14]Stendahl, *Final Account*, 42–43.

tend not to care that much about the statistics concerning the saved. (Other kinds of statistics, we care about deeply.) We are all the time asking how the world will be redeemed, and what our role in that redemption will be. In that, Paul is our spiritual kindred. Paul knew a God who was interested in human flourishing, justice, and inclusion, and I think progressive Christians know the same God. As someone who traveled the road before us, Paul has a lot to teach us.

I am not a theologian, and it will fall to someone else to make good theological sense of these different implications. However, having spent over fifteen years with one foot in progressive Christian congregations and the other foot in the discourse of the Radical New Perspective, I see the potential there for the renewal of Christian theology. Progressive Christians are often defined more by what they say they don't believe than they are by what they do believe, but escaping the Lutheran Perspective theologies and reading Paul anew through the New Perspective can provide new building blocks for new ways of being faithful and new ways of articulating that faithfulness, and for participating in the redemption of the world.

CHAPTER 9

Paul the Hijacker (A Conclusion)

I do not mean to suggest in this book that Paul was always a likeable or pleasant person. I think Paul was probably insufferable and a very difficult person with whom to get along. Paul seemed to anger nearly everybody he met. His boasting in 2 Corinthians 11 about the lashes and imprisonments and floggings he endured—that is not the kind of thing that happens repeatedly to most people. Based on the evidence we have, Peter and the rest of the Jerusalem apostles didn't like Paul. The so-called "super-apostles" in 2 Corinthians (11:5; 12:11) didn't seem to care for Paul, nor did his opponents in Galatia. Both his letters and the book of Acts contain stories about him getting chased out of town, and Galatians and 2 Corinthians are both evidence of how indignantly angry he could get. Paul had the wide-eyed, wild confidence of someone convinced he knew the truth, and he was constantly frustrated that he could not convince everyone else of that same truth. As is the case with so many other things, I think Krister Stendahl puts it best. "Paul was arrogant," he writes, "[b]ut he was so blatantly arrogant that one can somehow cope with it. He was always the greatest: the greatest of sinners, the greatest of apostles, the greatest when it came to speaking in tongues, the greatest at having been persecuted... Nobody could stand him—but he was great..."[1]

Paul might have been *the worst,* but not for the reasons we usually think. Paul has been branded as an oppressor of women, a hater of gay and lesbian people, an anti-Semite, and a prude, but I don't think any of those things were true. He has been blamed for defending slavery, used to defend nationalist xenophobia, and invoked as the foundation of a theological system that many people find stifling and dehumanizing, but I don't think he had much to do with any of those things. Paul could undoubtedly have been a difficult human being

---

[1]Krister Stendhal, *Final Account: Paul's Letter to the Romans* (Minneapolis: Fortress, 1995), 3.

to be around, but most of the things we think about him—*especially* most of the things progressive Christians think about him—have less to do with Paul and more to do with the ways Paul has been misread, misused, and misappropriated. The Christian tradition has betrayed Paul, and used his words to defend some of the worst aspects of church and society. I think if Paul were around today, he would flash some of his characteristic anger and flabbergasted shock at the way he has been interpreted.

I'm always skeptical when people are described as being "progressive for their time and place" or "ahead of their time," because it's usually a sign that some bad behavior is about to get explained away. However, in Paul's case, I think he was not only progressive for *his* time and place, he was progressive for *our* time and place. To return to one of the principles I outlined in the first chapter, it's important that we pay attention to Paul's *actions*. His actions reveal, again and again, a person who should be our ally. He empowered women and worked with them closely as leaders of congregations, and he relied on them as partners in mission. He proudly defended Judaism against gentile pride and the first inklings of what would become a long history of Christian anti-Semitism. Paul intervened on behalf of the slave Onesimus, even as he doubted the usefulness of changing one's social station when the world was so precariously close to ending. He affirmed different relationship models for different people, depending on their dispositions and needs. He spent his life traveling far from home in difficult conditions, desperately trying to do the thing he thought God had called him to do.

Some of the strongest evidence that Paul was sneakily progressive is the existence of the pseudo-Pauline literature. Years after Paul's death, as the Christian tradition was becoming more visible and more mainstream, people actually felt compelled to forge documents in his name to try to moderate his legacy—to put words into Paul's mouth about women obeying their husbands, slaves obeying their masters, and restrictions on sexual practices. Colossians, Ephesians, 1 Timothy, and the like exist *because* Paul was not sufficiently conservative for the tradition that followed. Paul didn't tell women to be silent and submissive in his own writings, or tell slaves to obey their masters, so someone did it for him.

The single most persistent charge that I hear progressive Christians make against Paul is that he hijacked Christianity. Jesus had left behind a tradition of love, healing, and equality, they say, and Paul came along and turned it into a religion full of regressive social policies, oppressive theology, and rules. People claim that Paul "added things" to Christianity, that he manipulated the tradition into something it was never meant to be, and that he cynically turned the religion *of* Jesus into a religion *about* Jesus. I don't think this is true, at least in the ways people usually mean. Paul was the first interpreter of Jesus whose writings we still have, and he has probably been the most influential. Christianity as it exists today definitely has a Pauline shape to it. However, the contours of that shape aren't the contours so many people assume.

Paul made two great and lasting contributions to the Christian tradition: his letters, and his orientation toward gentiles. His letters have been a deep well of theological resources, from the first century to the twenty-first, and Christian theology is unimaginable without him. Theologians from Augustine to Luther, to Nancy Ambrose and her grandson Howard Thurman, to thousands of others in between have crafted theology out of the raw materials left to them by Paul, by arguing with, against, or alongside him. Although he never meant for them to become so, Paul's letters have been the engine that has driven Christian theology through reformations, restorations, rebellions, and equilibrium. Although he could not have anticipated it, his writings in response to the Galatians' inconstancy have fueled Jewish-Christian dialogue, his passionate letters to the Corinthians have produced Christian ethics, and his letter to the Romans asking for help getting to Spain has stood as the towering document of the Christian tradition. Paul's letters have gained life beyond any he could have imagined, and they will continue to animate, vex, and inspire the church for centuries to come.

Paul might not have been the only apostle to the gentiles—his letters to the Galatians and the Corinthians suggest that he was not— but he was without question the most important. It was Paul who insisted that God intended Jesus to mean something beyond Israel, and it was Paul who "opposed Cephas to his face" (Gal. 2:11) when Peter wavered at the inclusion of gentiles in the Jesus movement. This is a complicated legacy—it has given birth to centuries of bloody Christian anti-Semitism—but Paul was arguing just as vigorously for gentile humility before the Jews as he was for Jewish inclusion of the gentiles. The riots, the pogroms, and the Holocaust belong to Christianity and to the interpreters of Paul, but they do not belong to Paul. He envisioned that, in the last days, God was creating an opening, a place among the bent branches of Israel, where gentiles could be grafted in. In this matter, he pleaded for grace from both Jews and gentiles.

Sometimes when I am talking with other scholars of Paul, conversation turns to how much we over-identify with the apostle.

We see ourselves in him, or at least we see ourselves as we would like to imagine we are. We relate to Paul's impertinence, his impatience, and his righteous indignation, and we admire his high-mindedness alongside his knack for an angry tirade. Paul embodies the expansive inclusiveness that we would like to embody, and he is faithful to a particularity that we appreciate. He stood absolutely on principle, but bent himself to the situation. He was all things to all people. But, if you could have asked him, I'm sure he would have said he was, above all, an apostle of Jesus Christ—an apostle to the gentiles.

That is why I have written this book—to convince you that you, the reader, might see Paul this way too. This way of seeing him does not overlook or eradicate the many ways Paul's name has been used in violence, but it does see him for what he was: a strident, prideful, complicated, and arrogant man, but also a religious visionary, a proud Jew, a defender of the poor and the weak, a colleague to women, and a man so possessed by a vision and a call that he gladly turned his life over to it. I think of him as my ally in the struggles I believe in, and I hope you will too.

Bibliography

Avery-Peck, Alan J. "Notes on The Second Letter of Paul to the
  Corinthians." In *The Jewish Annotated New Testament,* edited by
  Amy-Jill Levine and Marc Zvi Brettler. Second Edition. Oxford:
  Oxford, 2017.

Augustine of Hippo. *City of God.* Translated by Henry Bettenson.
  London: Penguin, 2003.

Betz, Hans Dieter. *Galatians.* Hermeneia—A Critical and Historical
  Commentary on the Bible. Minneapolis: Fortress Press, 1979.

Byrd, James P. *Sacred Scripture, Sacred War: The Bible and the American
  Revolution.* New York: Oxford University Press, 2013.

Coogan, Michael D. *A Brief Introduction to the Old Testament.* New York
  and Oxford: Oxford University Press, 2009.

Dibelius, Martin, and Hans Conzelmann. *The Pastoral Epistles.*
  Hermeneia—A Critical and Historical Commentary on the
  Bible. Minneapolis: Fortress Press, 1989.

Dunn, James D. G. "The Justice of God: A Renewed Perspective on
  Justification by Faith." *The Journal of Theological Studies* 43, no.
  1 (April 1992): 1–22.

———. *The Theology of Paul the Apostle.* Grand Rapids, Mich.: Wm. B.
  Eerdmans, 1998.

Ehrman, Bart D. *Forged: Writing in the Name of God—Why the Bible's
  Authors Are Not Who We Think They Are.* San Francisco: Harper
  Collins, 2011.

———. *Forgery and Counterforgery: The Use of Literary Deceit in Early
  Christian Polemics.* Oxford: Oxford University Press, 2013.

Eisenbaum, Pamela. *Paul Was Not a Christian: The Original Message of a
  Misunderstood Apostle.* New York: HarperOne, 2009.

Elliott, Neil. *The Arrogance of Nations: Reading Romans in the Shadow of
  Empire.* Paul in Critical Contexts. Minneapolis: Fortress Press,
  2008.

_____. "Romans." In *A Postcolonial Commentary on the New Testament Writings*, edited by Segovia, Fernando F. and R.S. Sugirtharajah. London: T & T Clark, 2009.

Epp, Eldon Jay. *Junia: The First Woman Apostle*. Minneapolis: Augsburg Fortress, 2005.

Finer, Lawrence B. "Trends in Premarital Sex in the United States, 1954–2003." *Public Health Reports* 122, no. 1 (2007): 73–78.

Franklin, Rosie. "True Love Doesn't Wait." *Disrupting Dinner Parties: Feminism for Everyone* (blog), March 22, 2013. https://disruptingdinnerparties.com/2013/03/22/truelovedoesntwait/.

Harrison, James R. "Virtues and Vices: New Testament Ethical Exhortation in Its Graeco-Roman Context." In *Oxford Bibliographies*. Oxford University Press, May 24, 2017. DOI: 10.1093/OBO/9780195393361-0236.

Hays, Richard B. *The Faith of Jesus Christ: The Narrative Substructure of Galatians 3:1—4:11*. Second Edition. The Biblical Resource Series. Grand Rapids: Wm. B. Eerdmans, 2002.

Jewett, Robert. *Romans: A Commentary*. Hermeneia—A Critical and Historical Commentary on the Bible. Minneapolis: Fortress, 2007.

King, Martin Luther, Jr. "Letter from a Birmingham City Jail," April 16, 1963. https://kinginstitute.stanford.edu/king-papers/documents/letter-birmingham-jail.

Koltun-Fromm, Naomi. "The First Letter of Paul to Timothy." In *The Jewish Annotated New Testament,* edited by Amy-Jill Levine and Marc Zvi Brettler. Second Edition. Oxford: Oxford University Press, 2017.

Lander, Shira. "Notes on 1 Corinthians." In *The Jewish Annotated New Testament,* edited by Amy-Jill Levine and Marc Zvi Brettler. Second Edition. Oxford: Oxford University Press, 2017.

Levine, Amy-Jill, and Marc Zvi Brettler, eds. *Jewish Annotated New Testament*. Second Edition. Oxford: Oxford University Press, 2017.

Luther, Martin. "Preface to the Letter of St. Paul to the Romans." Translated by Bro. Andrew Thornton, OSB, n.d. https://www.ccel.org/l/luther/romans/pref_romans.html.

MacDonald, Margaret Y. "Reading Real Women through the Undisputed Letters of Paul." In *Women & Christian Origins*, edited by Ross Shepard Kraemer and Mary Rose D'Angelo.

Oxford: Oxford University Press, 1999.

Martin, Dale B. *The Corinthian Body*. New Haven, Conn.: Yale University Press, 1995.

Massachusetts Anti-Slavery Society. *Annual Report Presented to the Massachusetts Anti-Slavery Society by Its Board of Managers*. Massachusetts Anti-Slavery Society, 1851.

Mayhew, Jonathan. "A Discourse Concerning Unlimited Submission and Non-Resistance to the Higher Powers: With Some Reflections on the Resistance Made to King Charles I. And on the Anniversary of His Death: In Which the Mysterious Doctrine of That Prince's Saintship" (1750), edited by Paul Royster,. *DigitalCommons@University of Nebraska - Lincoln*, https://digitalcommons.unl.edu/cgi/viewcontent.cgi?referer=https://www.google.com/&httpsredir=1&article=1044&context=etas .

McGuckin, John Anthony, ed. *The Westminster Handbook to Origen*. The Westminster Handbooks to Christian Theology. Louisville: Westminster John Knox, 2004.

Miller, Emily McFarlan, and Yonat Shimron, "Why Is Jeff Sessions Quoting Romans 13 and Why Is the Bible Verse so Often Invoked?" *USA Today*. Accessed September 14, 2018. https://www.usatoday.com/story/news/2018/06/16/jeff-sessions-bible-romans-13-trump-immigration-policy/707749002/.

Mukuka, Tarcisius. "Reading/Hearing Romans 13:1–7 under an African Tree: Towards a Lectio Postcolonica Contexta Africana." *New Testament Society of Southern Africa* 46, no. 1 (2012): 105–38.

Mullen, Lincoln. "The Fight to Define Romans 13." *The Atlantic*, June 15, 2018. https://www.theatlantic.com/ideas/archive/2018/06/romans-13/562916/.

Nanos, Mark. "Notes on Romans." In *The Jewish Annotated New Testament*, edited by Amy-Jill Levine and Marc Zvi Brettler. Second Edition. Oxford: Oxford University Press, 2017.

Nordling, Cherith Fee. "Gender." In *The Oxford Handbook of Evangelical Theology*, edited by Gerald R. McDermott. Oxford: Oxford University Press, 2010.

Origen. *Commentary on the Epistle to the Romans, Books 6—10*. Translated by Thomas P. Scheck. Washington, D.C.: Catholic University of America Press, 2002.

Powery, Emerson B., and Rodney S. Sadler Jr. *The Genesis of Liberation: Biblical Interpretation in the Antebellum Narratives of the Enslaved*. Louisville: Westminster John Knox, 2016.

Sanders, E. P. *Paul and Palestinian Judaism: A Comparison of Patterns of Religion*. Philadelphia: Fortress, 1977.

Singgih, Emanuel Gerrit. "Towards a Postcolonial Interpretation of Romans 13:1–7: Karl Barth, Robert Jewett and the Context of Reformation in Present-Day Indonesia." *Asia Journal of Theology* 23, no. 1 (April 2009): 111–22.

Stendahl, Krister. *Final Account: Paul's Letter to the Romans*. Minneapolis: Fortress, 1995.

_____. "Paul and the Introspective Conscience of the West." In *Paul Among Jews and Gentiles*, 78–96. Philadelphia: Fortress, 1976.

Stowers, Stanley K. *A Rereading of Romans: Justice, Jews, and Gentiles*. New Haven: Yale University, 1994.

Sunshine, Glenn S. *A Brief Introduction to the Reformation*. Louisville: Westminster John Knox Press, 2017.

Thurman, Howard. *Jesus and the Disinherited*. Nashville: Abingdon-Cokesbury Press, 1949.

"The Fugitive Slave Law." *Weekly North Carolina Standard*. October 30, 1850.

Zaas, Peter. "The Letter of Paul to the Colossians." In *The Jewish Annotated New Testament,* edited by Amy-Jill Levine and Marc Zvi Brettler. Oxford: Oxford University Press, 2017.